EDITOR: Maryanne Blacker

FOOD EDITOR: Pamela Clark

• • •

DESIGNER: Robbylee Phelan

• • •

ASSISTANT FOOD EDITORS: Kathy Snowball, Louise Patniotis

ASSOCIATE FOOD EDITOR: Enid Morrison

SENIOR HOME ECONOMISTS: Kathy McGarry, Sophia Young

HOME ECONOMISTS: Myles Beaufort, Cynthia Black, Leisel Chen, Bronwen Clark, Caroline Jones

EDITORIAL COORDINATOR: Elizabeth Hooper

KITCHEN ASSISTANT: Amy Wong

• • •

STYLISTS: Lucy Andrews, Wendy Berecry, Carolyn Fienberg, Jane Hann, Rosemary de Santis

PHOTOGRAPHERS: Mark Bramley, Kevin Brown, Robert Clark, Robert Taylor, Jon Waddy

• • •

HOME LIBRARY STAFF:

ASSISTANT EDITOR: Bridget van Tinteren

ART DIRECTOR: Sue de Guingand

EDITORIAL COORDINATOR: Fiona Lambrou

• • •

ACP PUBLISHER: Richard Walsh

ACP DEPUTY PUBLISHER: Nick Chan

• • •

We would like to thank Carol Selva Rajah for her advice on Malaysian recipe names and cultural notes.

Produced by The Australian Women's Weekly Home Library. Typeset by ACP Colour Graphics Pty Ltd. Colour separations by Network Graphics Pty. Ltd. in Sydney. Printing by Diamond Press Holdings Pty. Ltd. in Sydney. Published by ACP Publishing Pty Ltd, 54 Park Street, Sydney.
♦ **AUSTRALIA:** Distributed by Network Distribution Company, 54 Park Street Sydney, (02) 282 8777.
♦ **UNITED KINGDOM:** Distributed in the U.K. by Australian Consolidated Press (UK) Ltd, 20 Galowhill Rd, Brackmills, Northampton NN4 OEE (0604) 760 456.
♦ **CANADA:** Distributed in Canada by Whitecap Books Ltd, 1086 West 3rd St, North Vancouver B.C. V7P 3J6 (604) 980 9852.
♦ **NEW ZEALAND:** Distributed in New Zealand by Netlink Distribution Company, 17B Hargreaves St, Level 5, College Hill, Auckland 1 (9) 302 7616.
♦ **SOUTH AFRICA:** Distributed in South Africa by Intermag, PO Box 57394, Springfield 2137 (011) 493 3200.

• • •

Easy Malaysian-Style Cookery

Includes index.
ISBN 1 86396 019 8

1. Cookery, Malaysian. I Title: Australian Women's Weekly. (Series: Australian Women's Weekly Home Library).

641.59595

• • •

© A C P Publishing Pty Ltd 1994
ACN 053 273 546

• • •

COVER: Stir-Fried Vegetables, page 36.
OPPOSITE: Pandan Chiffon Cake, page 120.
BACK COVER: Potatoes and Noodles with Chilli Vegetables, page 27.

Easy Malaysian-Style *Cookery*

Conveniently positioned in the heart of Asia, Malaysia offers an exotic mix of culinary delights – a cuisine heavily influenced by people from India, China, Indonesia and Sri Lanka who have all settled there. A wide variety of produce is used in the cooking – from tropical fruit and vegetables, rice, grains, meats and every type of seafood imaginable to a generous use of coconut milk, belacan, tamarind and different blends of spices. Traditionally, food is eaten with the hands but with the colonial influence of the Portuguese came the use of knives and forks. Malaysian food can be quite fiery; adjust the quantity of chillies as desired. Occasionally, we have used an ingredient that may not be strictly authentic, but the completed recipes truly give you a taste of the fabulous flavours Malaysia has to offer.

Pamela Clark

FOOD EDITOR

BRITISH & NORTH AMERICAN READERS: Please note that Australian cup and spoon measurements are metric. A quick conversion guide appears on page 127. A glossary explaining unfamiliar terms and ingredients appears on page 122.

Snacks & Soups

HIDANGAN RINGAN DAN SUPS

Entrees served before the main meal are unheard of in Malaysia but there is a period before dinner when drinks and small eats (makan kecil) may be served. These enticing snacks, sold at street stalls or by passing vendors, can also be part of the main meal, or served as savoury snacks with tea; everyone stops for a cup of tea and snacks in the late afternoon to curb hunger pangs as dinner is served late, about 9pm. Soups, served as part of the main meal, are eaten with rice in between mouthfuls of spicy curries and sambals to cool the palate and provide a variety of tastes and textures.

CURRIED DHAL AND PRAWN CAKES

UADAI UDANG

1½ cups (300g) brown lentils
150g uncooked prawns, shelled, finely chopped
6 green shallots, chopped
2 small fresh red chillies, chopped
2 teaspoons mild curry powder
1 egg yolk, lightly beaten
1 clove garlic, crushed
plain flour
vegetable oil for deep-frying

2. Combine lentils, prawns, shallots, chillies, curry powder, egg yolk and garlic in bowl; mix well.

1. Place lentils in bowl, cover well with cold water, cover, stand overnight. Drain lentils, rinse under cold water. Blend or process lentils in 2 batches until smooth.

3. Using floured hands, shape ¼ cup (60ml) mixture into balls, flatten slightly, roll in flour.

4. Deep-fry prawn cakes in hot oil until browned and cooked through; drain on absorbent paper. Serve with mango sambal (see recipe on page 43), if desired.

Makes about 12.

- Prawn cakes can be prepared several hours ahead.
- Storage: Covered, in refrigerator.
- Freeze: Uncooked prawn cakes suitable.
- Microwave: Not suitable.

Place mats and baskets from Accoutrement.

2. Divide dough in half, roll each half into a log shape. Cut each log into 8 pieces. Flatten each piece with the palm of hand, roll out to 10cm rounds. Place 1½ tablespoons of filling in centre of each round, gather edges together, twist firmly.

3. Place buns, gathered side up, on baking paper in bamboo steamer; do not have buns touching. Cook, covered, over wok or pan of simmering water about 15 minutes, or until firm.

STEAMED PORK BUNS

BAK POW

2 cups (300g) plain flour
3 teaspoons baking powder
1 tablespoon caster sugar
1 tablespoon vegetable oil
¾ cup (180ml) warm water

FILLING
400g barbecued pork, chopped
2 medium (60g) Chinese sausages,
**   chopped**
2 teaspoons soy sauce
2 teaspoons oyster sauce
1 tablespoon sugar
2 teaspoons sesame oil
¼ cup (60ml) peanut butter
¼ cup (35g) cornflour
1 tablespoon vegetable oil
1 tablespoon chopped fresh
**   garlic chives**
1 tablespoon hoi sin sauce

1. Sift dry ingredients into bowl, gradually stir in oil and water; mix to a soft dough. Press dough into a ball, knead gently on lightly floured surface until smooth, cover, stand 10 minutes.

4. Filling: Combine all ingredients in bowl; mix well. Cover, stand 1 hour.

Makes 16.

■ Recipe best made just before serving.
■ Freeze: Suitable.
■ Microwave: Not suitable.

Basket from Java Bazaar.

CHICKEN AND CORN SOUP

SAP AYAM DAN JAGONG

200g minced chicken
1 egg white
2 tablespoons water
440g can creamed corn
3 cups (750ml) chicken stock
1 teaspoon soy sauce
1 teaspoon sesame oil
1½ tablespoons cornflour
¼ cup (60ml) water, extra

1. Combine chicken, egg white and water in bowl; mix well, stand 10 minutes.

2. Combine corn, stock, sauce and oil in pan, stir over heat until boiling, simmer, uncovered, 3 minutes. Stir in blended cornflour and extra water. Cook, stirring, until soup boils and thickens. Add chicken mixture, cook, stirring, 2 minutes.

Serves 4.

▦ Recipe can be made a day ahead.
▦ Storage: Covered, in refrigerator.
▦ Freeze: Not suitable.
▦ Microwave: Not suitable.

Tray from Accoutrement.

SOUR FISH SOUP

SUP IKAN MASIN

2 teaspoons grated fresh galangal
3 stems fresh lemon grass, chopped
2 small fresh red chillies
1 tablespoon grated fresh ginger
1.5 litres (6 cups) fish stock
400g boneless white fish fillets
1/3 cup (80ml) lime juice
2 fresh kaffir lime leaves,
finely shredded
1 tablespoon shredded fresh
mint leaves
mint leaves, extra

1. Blend or process galangal, lemon grass, chillies and ginger until finely chopped. Bring stock to boil, add chilli mixture, simmer, covered, 30 minutes.

2. Chop fish into 2cm pieces. Just before serving, add fish, juice, leaves and mint to pan, cook, uncovered, about 5 minutes or until fish is just tender. Serve with extra mint leaves.

Serves 4.

▓ Recipe can be prepared a day ahead.
▓ Storage: Covered, in refrigerator.
▓ Freeze: Not suitable.
▓ Microwave: Suitable.

Bowls from Accoutrement.

CURRIED LAMB PASTRIES

MURTABAK

3 cups (450g) plain flour
20g ghee
1 cup (250ml) warm water
1 tablespoon warm water,
    approximately, extra
2 cups (500ml) vegetable oil
50g ghee, extra

FILLING
30g ghee
1 medium (150g) onion,
    finely chopped
3 cloves garlic, crushed
½ teaspoon sambal oelek
1 tablespoon grated fresh ginger
1½ tablespoons mild curry powder
1 tablespoon garam masala
500g minced lamb
2 tablespoons chopped
    fresh coriander
2 tablespoons chopped fresh mint
3 eggs, lightly beaten

1. Sift flour into bowl, rub in ghee. Stir in water and enough extra water to form a soft dough. Turn dough onto lightly floured surface, knead about 10 minutes or until very smooth and elastic.

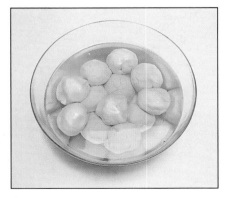

2. Divide dough into 12 portions, roll each portion into a ball. Place balls in bowl, pour oil over balls, cover, stand 1 hour.

3. Spread a little of the oil over a smooth surface, press out a drained dough ball until a very thin 24cm square. Place ¼ cup (60ml) of filling in centre of square, spread filling to 10cm square. Fold in sides of dough to form a parcel; trim overlapping edges if too thick. Repeat with remaining dough balls and filling.

4. Heat extra ghee in pan, cook parcels until well browned on both sides; drain on absorbent paper. Serve immediately.

5. Filling: Heat ghee in pan, add onion, garlic, sambal oelek and ginger, cook, stirring, until onion is soft. Stir in spices, stir until fragrant. Add mince, cook, stirring, until well browned; stir in herbs; cool. Stir in eggs.

Makes 12.

- Filling can be made a day ahead.
- Storage: Covered, in refrigerator.
- Freeze: Not suitable.
- Microwave: Not suitable.

SPICY FISH CAKES IN BANANA LEAVES

OTAK OTAK

Banana leaves need to be ordered from a fruit and vegetable shop or Asian food store. Usually, 1 banana leaf can be cut into 10 pieces. Remove main stem as it is not suitable to use.

6 fresh kaffir lime leaves, chopped
1 stem fresh lemon grass, chopped
8 green shallots, chopped
1 teaspoon belacan
1 teaspoon grated fresh turmeric
3 small fresh red chillies, chopped
½ teaspoon freshly ground
    black pepper
¼ cup firmly packed fresh
    coriander leaves
350g boneless firm white fish
    fillets, chopped
2 eggs, lightly beaten
½ cup (125ml) coconut milk
banana leaf
bottled chilli sauce

1. Process lime leaves, lemon grass, shallots, belacan, turmeric, chillies, pepper and coriander until finely chopped. Add fish, process until just combined.

2. Combine fish mixture and eggs in bowl, mix well. Gradually stir in coconut milk; mix well.

3. Cut banana leaf into 8 x 20cm squares. Immerse squares in large pan of boiling water, remove immediately, rinse under cold water, pat dry with absorbent paper. Leaf should be soft and pliable. Repeat with remaining squares.

4. Place ⅓ cup (80ml) of fish mixture in centre of each square. Lift 2 sides of leaf and fold towards centre, repeat with other sides to form a parcel. Secure with string.

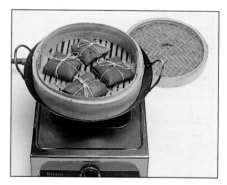

5. Place parcels in a single layer in bamboo steamer, cook, covered, over wok or pan of boiling water about 10 minutes or until fish mixture is firm. Serve parcels with bottled chilli sauce.

Makes 8.

- Recipe best made on day of serving.
- Storage: Covered, in refrigerator.
- Freeze: Not suitable.
- Microwave: Not suitable.

Banana leaf bowl from Java Bazaar.

BEEF CURRY PUFFS

KARI PAP DAGING

1 tablespoon vegetable oil
1 small (80g) onion, finely chopped
1 small (120g) potato, finely chopped
2 teaspoons finely grated fresh ginger
2 cloves garlic, crushed
4 green shallots, finely chopped
150g minced beef
1 tablespoon mild curry powder
⅓ cup (80ml) coconut cream
1½ cups (225g) plain flour
100g butter, chopped
1 egg yolk
2 tablespoons lemon juice,
    approximately
1 egg, lightly beaten

1. Heat oil in pan, add onion, cook, stirring, until onion is soft. Add potato, ginger, garlic, shallots and mince, cook, stirring, until mince is browned and potato tender. Add curry powder and cream; mix well; cool.

2. Sift flour into bowl, rub in butter. Add egg yolk and enough juice to form a soft dough. Press dough into a ball, knead gently on lightly floured surface until smooth, cover, refrigerate 30 minutes.

3. Roll dough between 2 sheets of baking paper to 3mm thickness. Cut dough into 12 x 12cm rounds. Spoon 1½ tablespoons of mince mixture onto

centre of each round; brush edges with beaten egg. Fold pastry over filling; seal edges with a fork.

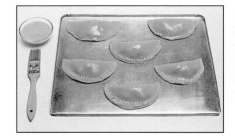

4. Place curry puffs on greased oven trays, brush with remaining beaten egg, bake in hot oven 10 minutes. Reduce heat to moderate, bake further 20 minutes or until browned.

Makes 12.

- Puffs best cooked just before serving. Mince mixture can be made a day ahead.
- Storage: Covered, in refrigerator.
- Freeze: Uncooked puffs suitable.
- Microwave: Mince mixture suitable.

Pewter dish and bamboo tray from Accoutrement.

SPICY PORK ROLLS

LOBAK

1 tablespoon vegetable oil
1 small (200g) leek, chopped
500g minced pork
1 egg
½ teaspoon five spice powder
2 teaspoons soy sauce
½ teaspoon sesame oil
1 beancurd sheet
vegetable oil for deep-frying

1. Heat oil in pan, add leek, cook, stirring, until leek is soft; drain on absorbent paper. Combine leek, pork, egg, spice powder, sauce and sesame oil in bowl; mix well.

2. Dip beancurd sheet into bowl of cold water, cut into 8 rectangles 12cm x 22cm. Place ¼ cup (60ml) of mince mixture in a 15cm long sausage along 1 end of the beancurd rectangle. Brush edges lightly with water. Fold sides in and roll up, wet the join and press down firmly to seal.

3. Deep-fry rolls in hot oil until well browned and mince is cooked through. Serve sliced with chilli sauce, if desired.

Makes 8.
■ Recipe can be prepared a day ahead.
■ Storage: Covered, in refrigerator.
■ Freeze: Not suitable.
■ Microwave: Not suitable.

China from Villeroy & Boch.

2. Chop prawns very finely. Combine prawns, mince, sesame oil, garlic, egg white, breadcrumbs and blended cornflour and extra sauce in bowl; mix well. With damp hands, roll tablespoons of mixture into balls.

3. Bring reserved prawn liquid to boil, add pork balls, boil, uncovered, about 8 minutes or until balls float to surface and are cooked.

PORK AND BEANCURD SOUP

PONG TAUHU

500g uncooked medium prawns
1½ tablespoons vegetable oil
2 cloves garlic, sliced
1.5 litres (6 cups) water
1 tablespoon fish sauce
1 tablespoon soy sauce
250g minced pork
½ teaspoon sesame oil
1 clove garlic, crushed
1 egg white
⅓ cup (25g) stale breadcrumbs
1 teaspoon cornflour
1 teaspoon soy sauce, extra
130g soft beancurd, thinly sliced
3 Chinese cabbage leaves, chopped
2 green shallots, chopped
¼ cup (50g) canned drained bamboo
  shoots, thinly sliced
¼ cup (25g) packaged fried onions

1. Shell and devein prawns. Rinse shells and heads several times in cold water until water is clear, drain; pat dry with absorbent paper. Heat vegetable oil in wok or pan, add shells and garlic, cook, stirring, until shells change colour. Add water and sauces, bring to boil; remove from heat. Drain, reserve liquid, discard shells.

4. Just before serving, stir in beancurd, cabbage, shallots and bamboo shoots, cook until heated through. Serve soup topped with fried onions.

Serves 6.

▦ Recipe can be prepared a day ahead.
▦ Storage: Covered, in refrigerator.
▦ Freeze: Not suitable.
▦ Microwave: Not suitable.

Blue and white bowls from Accoutrement.

PRAWN CAKES

PENDARAM UDANG

1 tablespoon ground coriander
2 teaspoons ground cumin
½ teaspoon ground turmeric
1 medium (150g) onion, chopped
3 cloves garlic, crushed
2 tablespoons grated fresh ginger
500g uncooked prawns,
    shelled, chopped
1 tablespoon chopped fresh chives
2 tablespoons coconut cream
½ cup (75g) rice flour
rice flour, extra
vegetable oil for deep-frying

1. Combine coriander, cumin and turmeric in dry pan, stir over low heat until fragrant; cool.

2. Process onion, garlic, ginger, prawns and coriander mixture until well combined. Add chives, cream and rice flour, process until combined.

3. Using floured hands, shape 2 level tablespoons of mixture into flat cakes. Toss cakes in extra rice flour; shake away excess flour.

4. Deep-fry cakes in hot oil until well browned; drain on absorbent paper. Serve cakes with mild sweet chilli sauce, if desired.

Makes about 12.

▦ Recipe can be prepared a day ahead.
▦ Storage: Covered, in refrigerator.
▦ Freeze: Uncooked cakes suitable.
▦ Microwave: Not suitable.

2. Heat oil in wok or pan, add garlic, ginger and bamboo shoots, cook, stirring, until fragrant. Add mushrooms, yam bean, carrot and beancurd, cook, stirring, 1 minute; remove from heat. Combine sambal oelek, cabbage and blended cornflour and soy sauce in bowl; mix well. Stir in vegetable mixture, cool.

3. Spoon tablespoons of vegetable mixture across corners of spring roll wrappers. Brush edges with a little water, tuck in ends, roll up to enclose filling.

4. Deep-fry spring rolls in batches in hot oil until golden brown and cooked through; drain on absorbent paper.

Makes about 20.

- Recipe best made on day of serving.
- Storage: Covered, in refrigerator.
- Freeze: Uncooked rolls suitable.
- Microwave: Not suitable.

China from Villeroy & Boch; statue and fabric from Java Bazaar.

VEGETABLE SPRING ROLLS

POH PIA

6 Chinese dried mushrooms
1 tablespoon vegetable oil
2 cloves garlic, crushed
1 tablespoon grated fresh ginger
¼ cup (50g) canned drained bamboo shoots, finely chopped
½ medium (200g) yam bean, grated
1 medium (120g) carrot, grated
130g soft beancurd, thinly sliced
½ teaspoon sambal oelek
4 Chinese cabbage leaves, shredded
1 teaspoon cornflour
2 teaspoons soy sauce
½ x 200g packet (12.5cm square) spring roll wrappers
vegetable oil for deep-frying

1. Place mushrooms in heatproof bowl, cover with boiling water, stand 20 minutes. Drain mushrooms; discard stems, slice caps thinly.

PORK DUMPLINGS

WUN TUN

4 Chinese dried mushrooms
200g diced pork
1 clove garlic, crushed
½ small (60g) green cucumber,
**   seeded, grated**
½ small (35g) carrot, grated
1 teaspoon brown sugar
1 teaspoon rice wine vinegar
1 tablespoon cornflour
½ teaspoon sesame oil
1 egg, lightly beaten
30 gow gee pastry rounds
vegetable oil for deep-frying

CHILLI SAUCE
½ teaspoon vegetable oil
1 clove garlic, crushed
½ teaspoon finely chopped
**   fresh red chilli**
¼ cup (60ml) water
1 teaspoon rice wine vinegar
1 teaspoon sugar
½ teaspoon lime juice

1. Place mushrooms in heatproof bowl, cover with boiling water, stand 20 minutes. Drain mushrooms; discard stems, chop caps.

2. Process mushrooms and pork until finely minced. Combine pork mixture, garlic, cucumber, carrot, sugar, vinegar, cornflour, oil and egg in bowl; mix well.

3. Place 2 level teaspoons of mixture in centre of each pastry round, brush edges with water. Pull up edges of pastry around mixture, pinch together to seal.

4. Deep-fry dumplings in hot oil until lightly browned and cooked through (or, steam dumplings over simmering water about 10 minutes); drain on absorbent paper. Serve dumplings with chilli sauce.

5. Chilli Sauce: Heat oil in pan, add garlic and chilli, cook, stirring, 1 minute. Stir in combined water, vinegar and sugar, cool. Stir in juice.

Makes 30.

▦ Dumplings best made close to serving.
▦ Freeze: Uncooked dumplings suitable.
▦ Microwave: Sauce suitable.

Rice, Noodles & Bread

NASI, MEE DAN ROTI

Rice is a staple of the Malaysian people's diet; bowls of steaming rice are served with most meals, in some communities even at breakfast. Noodles, too, are everyday favourites and Malaysians have devised special noodle dishes which are spiced and seasoned to complement side dishes and soups. The famous soup, Laksa, evolved as a seafood curry ladled over noodles. Other popular side dishes are the Indian-style breads and pancakes.

PUFFED BREAD

ROTI CANAI

Serve hot with a curry or dhal.

3 cups (450g) plain flour
1 teaspoon sugar
1 egg
¾ cup (180ml) warm water, approximately
100g ghee, melted, approximately

1. Sift flour and sugar into bowl, stir in egg and enough water to mix to a soft dough. Turn dough onto lightly floured surface, knead about 10 minutes or until smooth and elastic. Cover dough with plastic wrap, stand 2 hours.

2. Divide dough into 12 portions. Roll out 1 portion to 18cm circle. Brush circle with some of the ghee. Roll dough up tightly like a Swiss roll, then roll up both ends so that they meet in the centre. Repeat with remaining dough portions. While working with dough, keep other portions covered with plastic wrap to prevent them from drying out. If making ahead, brush rolls with a little ghee and cover with plastic wrap.

3. Roll out rolls on lightly floured surface to 17cm circles. Cook roti over high heat in heavy-based pan greased with ghee until puffed and lightly browned on both sides.
Makes 12.
■ Roti best cooked just before serving.
■ Freeze: Suitable.
■ Microwave: Not suitable.

Fabric and small bowl from Community Aid Abroad Shop.

CURRIED SEAFOOD SOUP

LAKSA

350g uncooked medium prawns
1/3 cup (80ml) vegetable oil
1 litre (4 cups) coconut milk
2½ cups (625ml) water,
    approximately
8 (100g) fish balls
3 pieces fried beancurd, thinly sliced
100g snow peas, sliced
2 cups (160g) bean sprouts
250g rice vermicelli noodles
25 (150g) drained bottled oysters
2 limes, sliced

CURRY PASTE
1 tablespoon chopped fresh
    lemon grass
1 tablespoon grated fresh turmeric
1 tablespoon mild curry powder
2 tablespoons grated fresh ginger
6 French shallots, halved
6 candlenuts
4 cloves garlic, halved
2 teaspoons sambal oelek
2 teaspoons belacan

1. Shell and devein prawns, leaving tails intact. Heat oil in wok or pan, add curry paste, cook, stirring, until fragrant. Add prawns, cook, stirring, 2 minutes.

2. Add combined coconut milk, water, fish balls and beancurd, bring to boil. Boil, steam or microwave snow peas and bean sprouts separately until just tender; drain.

3. Add noodles to pan of boiling water, boil, uncovered, until just tender; drain. Divide noodles between serving bowls; add coconut milk mixture, top with combined bean sprouts and snow peas, oysters and limes.

4. Curry Paste: Blend or process all ingredients until smooth.

Serves 4.

- Curry paste can be made 3 days ahead. Soup best made close to serving.
- Storage: Curry paste, covered, in refrigerator.
- Freeze: Curry paste suitable.
- Microwave: Vegetables suitable.

Fabric and spoon from Community Aid Abroad Shop.

YELLOW RICE WITH COCONUT AND TAMARIND

NASI ULAM

Serve as an accompaniment to curry.

2 tablespoons grated fresh turmeric
1 tablespoon tamarind paste
2 cups (400g) glutinous rice
¼ teaspoon black peppercorns
1 cup (250ml) coconut milk

1. Place turmeric and tamarind in piece of muslin and tie securely. Wash rice well, place in large bowl with turmeric bag, cover with water, cover, stand overnight, squeezing bag occasionally to release turmeric flavour. Drain and rinse rice; discard turmeric bag.

2. Place large piece of muslin in steamer. Combine rice with peppercorns in steamer, cook, covered, over wok or pan of boiling water about 20 minutes or until rice is just tender, remove from heat.

3. Combine rice and coconut milk in large bowl, return to steamer, cook further 10 minutes.

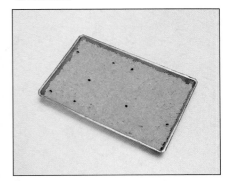

4. Grease 20cm x 30cm lamington pan. Press rice into prepared pan. Turn out and cut into squares when cold.

Serves 4.

▨ Rice must be soaked overnight. Recipe can be made a day ahead.
▨ Storage: Covered, in refrigerator.
▨ Freeze: Not suitable.
▨ Microwave: Not suitable.

Copper plate and basket from Accoutrement.

FISH, LIME AND PINEAPPLE SOUP

LAKSA PINANG

250g rice vermicelli noodles
2 teaspoons vegetable oil
600g snapper fillets, skinned,
    chopped
1½ cups (120g) bean sprouts
4 fresh kaffir lime leaves,
    finely shredded
½ small (400g) pineapple, chopped
1 small (130g) green cucumber,
    seeded, sliced
½ cup lightly packed fresh
    mint leaves
½ cup lightly packed fresh
    Vietnamese mint leaves

SPICE PASTE
1 tablespoon belacan
3 small fresh red chillies, chopped
1 medium (150g) onion, chopped
3 cloves garlic
6cm piece (100g) fresh galangal,
    chopped
2cm piece (30g) fresh turmeric,
    chopped
2 tablespoons chopped fresh
    lemon grass
1½ teaspoons sugar

STOCK
2kg fish heads
2 litres (8 cups) water
1 large (200g) onion, chopped
5cm piece (40g) fresh ginger,
    chopped
2 stems fresh lemon grass, chopped
1 large sprig fresh mint
1 large sprig fresh coriander,
    root intact
3 fresh kaffir lime leaves
2 large (500g) ripe tomatoes, chopped
60g tamarind paste

1. Add noodles to large pan of boiling water, boil, uncovered, until tender; drain, rinse under cold water, drain.

2. Heat oil in pan, add spice paste, cook, stirring, over low heat about 7 minutes or until fragrant. Add stock, simmer, uncovered, 10 minutes. Add fish, sprouts and lime leaves, simmer, uncovered, about 2 minutes or until fish is tender.

3. Divide noodles, pineapple, cucumber and mints between serving bowls, top with fish mixture.

4. Spice Paste: Add belacan to dry pan, cook until dry and crumbly. Blend or process belacan with remaining ingredients until well combined.

5. Stock: Wash fish heads well. Combine fish heads and remaining ingredients in large pan, simmer, uncovered, 30 minutes. Remove pan from heat, stand 15 minutes; strain. You will need 2 litres (8 cups) stock.

Serves 4 to 6.

- Spice paste and stock can be made a day ahead.
- Storage: Covered, in refrigerator.
- Freeze: Stock suitable.
- Microwave: Not suitable.

PORK AND PRAWNS WITH YELLOW NOODLES

MEE GORENG CINA

50g Chinese dried mushrooms
450g packet yellow noodles
4 green shallots
4 bunches (600g) choy sum
1 tablespoon vegetable oil
2 cloves garlic, crushed
1 tablespoon grated fresh ginger
4 small fresh red chillies,
**   seeded, chopped**
400g uncooked prawns,
**   shelled, chopped**
2 (350g) pork rump steaks, sliced
1 teaspoon cornflour
⅓ cup (80ml) soy sauce
2 tablespoons water

2. Add noodles to pan of boiling water, boil, uncovered, until tender; drain, rinse under cold water, drain well.

1. Place mushrooms in heatproof bowl, cover with boiling water, stand 20 minutes. Drain mushrooms, discard stems, slice caps.

3. Cut shallots and choy sum into 3cm lengths. Heat oil in wok or pan, add garlic, ginger, chillies, prawns and pork, stir-fry until prawns and pork are just tender. Add shallots, choy sum, mushrooms, noodles and blended cornflour, soy sauce and water. Stir over heat until choy sum is just wilted and liquid thickened slightly.

Serves 4.

▨ Recipe best made just before serving.
▨ Freeze: Not suitable.
▨ Microwave: Noodles suitable.

Bowl and tray from Accoutrement.

COCONUT MILK RICE

NASI LEMAK

Serve hot as an accompaniment.

1½ cups (300g) long-grain rice
1½ cups (375ml) water
1½ cups (375ml) coconut milk
3 green shallots, chopped
1 tablespoon grated fresh ginger

1. Rinse rice in strainer under cold water until water is clear. Combine rice, water and coconut milk in heavy-based pan; bring to boil, stirring, simmer gently 15 minutes, covered with a tight-fitting lid. Remove from heat, stand, covered, on a damp tea-towel 10 minutes. It is important not to remove lid during cooking and steaming process.

2. Fluff rice with a fork, gently stir through shallots and ginger.

Serves 4.

◼ Recipe can be made a day ahead.
◼ Storage: Covered, in refrigerator.
◼ Freeze: Suitable.
◼ Microwave: Not suitable.

TOMATO RICE

NASI TOMATO

Serve hot as an accompaniment.

125g ghee
8 French shallots, thinly sliced
1 medium (150g) onion,
  finely chopped
2 cloves garlic, crushed
¼ cup (50g) candlenuts,
  finely chopped
2 cinnamon sticks
2 star anise
2 cloves
2 cups (400g) long-grain rice
3 cups (750ml) boiling water
⅓ cup (80ml) tomato paste

1. Heat half the ghee in heavy-based pan, add shallots, cook, stirring, until lightly browned and crisp; drain on absorbent paper. Heat remaining ghee in same pan, add onion, garlic, candlenuts, cinnamon sticks, star anise and cloves, cook, stirring, until onion is soft.

2. Stir in rice, water and paste, simmer gently 15 minutes, covered with a tight-fitting lid. Remove from heat, stand, covered, on a damp tea-towel 10 minutes. It is important not to remove lid during cooking and standing process. Fluff rice with a fork. Discard spices, serve topped with shallots.

Serves 6.

▨ Recipe best made close to serving.
▨ Freeze: Not suitable.
▨ Microwave: Not suitable.

POTATOES AND NOODLES WITH CHILLI VEGETABLES

MEE GORENG INDIA

2 tablespoons grated fresh turmeric
400g baby potatoes, halved
300g flat rice noodles
2 eggs
1 tablespoon water
1 teaspoon vegetable oil
40g ghee
2 medium (300g) onions, sliced
2 medium (260g) tomatoes,
   halved, sliced
2 cups (160g) bean sprouts
8 Chinese cabbage leaves, shredded
2 tablespoons soy sauce
2 tablespoons tomato sauce

CHILLI PASTE
2 teaspoons sambal oelek
2 teaspoons belacan
4 cloves garlic, halved
4 French shallots, halved

1. Combine turmeric and potatoes in pan, add enough water to cover, cook, uncovered, until potatoes are just tender; drain. Place noodles in heatproof bowl, cover with boiling water, stand about 5 minutes or until just tender; drain.

2. Beat eggs and water together in bowl with fork. Heat oil in wok or pan, pour in egg mixture, cook, without stirring, until set. Remove omelette from wok, roll up firmly; slice thinly.

3. Heat ghee in clean wok or pan, add chilli paste, cook, stirring, until fragrant. Add onions, cook, stirring, until very soft. Add tomatoes, bean sprouts, cabbage and sauces, cook, stirring, about 2 minutes or until cabbage is just wilted.

4. Add potatoes, noodles and half the sliced omelette to vegetable mixture. Stir over heat until heated through; top with remaining omelette.

5. Chilli Paste: Blend or process all ingredients until finely chopped.

Serves 4 to 6.

- Chilli paste can be made 3 days ahead.
- Storage: Covered, in refrigerator.
- Freeze: Not suitable.
- Microwave: Not suitable.

2. Heat ghee in pan, add chicken and shallots, cook 3 minutes, add ginger mixture, ground almonds, cloves and cinnamon, cook, covered, 10 minutes, stirring occasionally.

3. Add yogurt, cook, uncovered, 10 minutes or until chicken is tender, discard cinnamon and cloves. Stir in coconut rice.

4. Coconut Rice: Rinse rice in strainer under cold water until water is clear. Combine rice, coconut cream and water in heavy-based pan, simmer gently for 15 minutes, covered with a tight-fitting lid. Remove from heat, stand, covered, on a damp tea-towel 10 minutes. It is important not to remove lid during cooking and steaming. Fluff rice with a fork.

Serves 4.

- ▇ Recipe best made just before serving.
- ▇ Freeze: Not suitable.
- ▇ Microwave: Not suitable.

Plate, bowls and tray from Accoutrement.

SPICED RICE WITH CHICKEN

NASI BIRYANI

1 clove garlic, crushed
5cm piece (40g) fresh ginger, chopped
2 small fresh red chillies, chopped
¼ cup (35g) cashews
¼ cup (40g) blanched almonds
20g ghee
8 chicken thigh cutlets
8 green shallots, chopped
1 tablespoon packaged ground almonds
5 cloves
1 cinnamon stick
1 cup (250ml) plain yogurt
COCONUT RICE
1½ cups (300g) long-grain rice
1 cup (250ml) coconut cream
1 cup (250ml) water

1. Blend or process garlic, ginger, chillies, cashews and blanched almonds until finely chopped.

PRAWN PATTIES WITH SPICY KUMARA SAUCE

BERGEDEL UDANG MASAK BEREMPAH

350g cooked shelled prawns
⅔ cup (100g) plain flour
1 egg
½ teaspoon baking powder
2 tablespoons vegetable oil
vegetable oil for deep-frying
150g kumara, chopped
1 cup (250ml) water
5 dried red chillies
3 candlenuts
2.5cm piece (45g) fresh galangal, peeled, chopped
1.5cm piece (20g) fresh turmeric, peeled, chopped
3 medium (450g) onions, chopped
2 tablespoons vegetable oil, extra
¼ cup (60ml) peanut butter
1 litre (4 cups) fish stock
300g fresh yellow noodles
2¼ cups (180g) bean sprouts

1. Blend or process prawns until finely minced, reserve 1 cup (200g) prawns for step 5. Combine remaining prawns, flour, egg, baking powder and oil in bowl; mix well.

2. Roll level teaspoons of prawn mixture into balls; flatten slightly to form patties. Deep-fry patties in batches in hot oil until lightly browned and cooked; drain on absorbent paper.

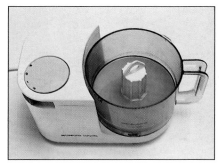

3. Boil, steam or microwave kumara until tender; process kumara and water until smooth.

4. Process chillies, candlenuts, galangal, turmeric and onions until finely minced. Heat extra oil in pan, add chilli mixture, cook, stirring, until fragrant.

5. Combine kumara mixture and chilli mixture in pan, add peanut butter, stock and reserved minced prawns. Stir in noodles, simmer 5 minutes, stir in prawn patties and bean sprouts, stir over heat until heated through.

Serves 4 to 6.

- Recipe can be made a day ahead.
- Storage: Covered, in refrigerator.
- Freeze: Suitable.
- Microwave: Kumara suitable.

Vegetables, Salads & Sambals

SAYUR SAYURAN, SALAD DAN SAMBAL

A variety of vegetables are often served as accompaniments to a main meal in Malaysia; usually cooked with spices, they are never dull in taste or appearance. Our recipes would also make delightful light meals on their own. Sambals, often fiery and fragrant with a sharp tang, are served in small dishes along with curries and mounds of rice. Our sambals range from mild to hot; it's best to sample them in small quantities until you find the heat that best suits your palate.

BRAISED CARROTS AND CABBAGE

KOBIS DAN LOBAK MERAH GORENG

1 teaspoon sesame oil
2 teaspoons ghee
½ teaspoon white mustard seeds
10 dried curry leaves
¼ medium (375g) cabbage,
**   finely shredded**
2 medium (240g) carrots, grated
2 tablespoons coconut
2 tablespoons vegetable oil
1 teaspoon sesame oil, extra
1 tablespoon soy sauce

1. Heat sesame oil and ghee in pan, add seeds, cook, stirring, until seeds begin to pop. Add leaves, cook, stirring, 1 minute.

2. Stir in cabbage and carrots, cook, covered, about 4 minutes or until vegetables are just tender. Add coconut, cook, stirring, 1 minute, remove from heat.

3. Combine vegetable oil, extra sesame oil and sauce in small bowl; mix well. Stir into vegetable mixture; mix well. Serve hot or cold.

Serves 4.

- Recipe can be made 3 hours before serving.
- Storage: Covered, in refrigerator.
- Freeze: Not suitable.
- Microwave: Not suitable.

1. Place noodles in heatproof bowl of boiling water, stand about 5 minutes or until noodles are soft; drain well. Shell and devein prawns.

2. Heat oil in pan, add chillies, turmeric, shallots and garlic, cook, stirring constantly, until fragrant.

3. Stir in coconut milk, water, cabbage, beans, cauliflower and prawns, simmer, uncovered, 2 minutes. Stir in coconut cream, noodles, tofu and fried soya bean cakes, simmer, uncovered, 3 minutes or until slightly thickened.

Serves 4.

▓ Recipe best made just before serving.
▓ Freeze: Not suitable.
▓ Microwave: Not suitable.

VEGETABLES IN COCONUT MILK

KUAH LONTONG

50g rice vermicelli noodles
150g medium uncooked prawns
2 tablespoons vegetable oil
3 small fresh red chillies,
   finely chopped
1 teaspoon ground turmeric
4 green shallots, finely chopped
3 cloves garlic, crushed
270ml can coconut milk

1 cup (250ml) water
2 cups (160g) shredded white
   cabbage
4 snake beans, chopped
1½ cups (150g) chopped cauliflower
140ml can coconut cream
50g piece firm tofu, sliced
220g packet fried soya bean
   cakes, halved

Box and bowl from Community Aid Abroad Shop.

VEGETABLES WITH CHILLI PEANUT SAUCE

ROJAK DAN KUAH KACANG

1 medium (120g) carrot, peeled
1 large (750g) yam bean, peeled
1 small (120g) green cucumber
¼ small (300g) cabbage
1 bunch (650g) English spinach

CHILLI PEANUT SAUCE
60g ghee
5 dried red chillies
6 green shallots, chopped
1 teaspoon belacan
2 teaspoons tamarind paste
1 tablespoon hot water
1 cup (150g) peanuts, roasted
½ cup (125ml) water, extra

3. Chilli Peanut Sauce: Heat ghee in pan or wok, add chillies, shallots and belacan, cook, stirring, until shallots are soft; drain on absorbent paper. Place tamarind and hot water in bowl; stand 10 minutes. Squeeze liquid from tamarind, strain and reserve liquid; discard tamarind.

4. Blend or process chilli mixture, reserved tamarind liquid and peanuts until fine. Add extra water, blend until combined.

Serves 6.

- Recipe can be made a day ahead.
- Storage: Covered, in refrigerator.
- Freeze: Not suitable.
- Microwave: Not suitable.

1. Cut carrot and yam bean into thick strips. Peel cucumber, remove seeds; cut cucumber into thick strips.

2. Cut cabbage into thick wedges. Trim stalks from spinach. Serve vegetables with chilli peanut sauce.

SPICY OKRA

KACANG BENDI

5 French shallots, halved
1 small fresh red chilli, chopped
2 cloves garlic, halved
1 teaspoon belacan
20g ghee
450g okra, halved
¾ cup (180ml) milk
½ cup (75g) plain flour
60g ghee, extra

1. Blend or process shallots, chilli, garlic and belacan until finely chopped. Heat ghee in pan or wok, add mixture, cook, stirring, until fragrant; remove from pan.

2. Combine okra and milk in bowl, drain; discard milk. Toss okra in flour. Heat extra ghee in pan, cook okra in batches until lightly browned; drain on absorbent paper.

3. Combine okra mixture and shallot mixture in bowl; mix well.

Serves 4 to 6.

- Recipe best made close to serving.
- Freeze: Not suitable.
- Microwave: Shallot mixture suitable.

Basket from Corso de Fiori; fabric from Community Aid Abroad Shop.

VEGETABLE SALAD WITH PEANUT SAUCE

GADO GADO

250g firm beancurd
vegetable oil for deep-frying
300g baby new potatoes, halved
10 (80g) snake beans, sliced
1 tablespoon sesame oil
2 teaspoons vegetable oil, extra
½ small (600g) cabbage
1 cup (80g) bean sprouts
1 small (130g) green cucumber,
    chopped
4 hard-boiled eggs

PEANUT SAUCE
1 cup (150g) peanuts, roasted
8 green shallots, chopped
2 cloves garlic, crushed
1 teaspoon belacan
1 small fresh red chilli, chopped
2 tablespoons vegetable oil
1 tablespoon palm sugar
1½ cups (375ml) coconut milk
½ cup (125ml) water

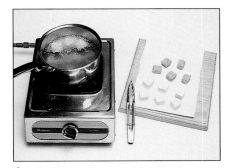

1. Cut beancurd into 2.5cm cubes, pat dry with absorbent paper. Deep-fry beancurd in batches in hot oil until browned; drain on absorbent paper.

2. Boil, steam or microwave potatoes and beans separately until just tender; drain, rinse under cold water, drain.

3. Heat sesame oil and extra vegetable oil in wok or pan, add cabbage, cook, stirring, until just tender; cool. Arrange cabbage, bean sprouts, beancurd, potatoes, beans, cucumber and eggs on large plate; drizzle with peanut sauce.

4. Peanut Sauce: Blend or process peanuts, shallots, garlic, belacan and chilli until smooth. Heat oil in pan, add peanut mixture, cook, stirring, 3 minutes, add sugar, coconut milk and water, simmer, uncovered, 3 minutes.

Serves 4.

- Recipe can be prepared several hours ahead.
- Storage: Covered, in refrigerator.
- Freeze: Not suitable.
- Microwave: Potatoes and beans suitable.

STIR-FRIED VEGETABLES

SAYUR MASAKAN CINA

30g Chinese dried mushrooms
1 medium (120g) carrot
2 teaspoons vegetable oil
2 teaspoons sesame oil
1 medium (150g) onion, sliced
2 cloves garlic, crushed
1 teaspoon grated fresh ginger
1 cup (125g) frozen peas, thawed
150g snow peas, sliced
1 medium (200g) red pepper, sliced
1 medium (200g) yellow
   pepper, sliced
4 green shallots, chopped
227g can bamboo shoots, drained
1½ tablespoons soy sauce
3 teaspoons oyster sauce
1½ tablespoons hoi sin sauce
3 teaspoons mild sweet chilli sauce

1. Place mushrooms in heatproof bowl, cover with boiling water, stand 20 minutes. Drain mushrooms; discard stems, slice caps. Cut carrot into thin strips. Boil, steam or microwave carrot strips until just tender.

2. Heat oils in wok or pan, add onion, garlic and ginger, cook, stirring, until onion is soft. Add mushrooms, carrot, peas, snow peas, peppers, shallots and bamboo shoots, cook, stirring, until vegetables are just tender. Add combined sauces, cook, stirring, until heated through.

Serves 4 to 6.

▦ Recipe can be prepared several hours ahead.
▦ Storage: Covered, in refrigerator.
▦ Freeze: Not suitable.
▦ Microwave: Carrot suitable.

Fabric from Community Aid Abroad Shop.

CHICKPEA CURRY

KARI KACANG DAHL

2 cups (400g) dried chickpeas
40g ghee
1 medium (150g) onion, sliced
1 tablespoon grated fresh galangal
3 small fresh red chillies, chopped
2 teaspoons ground cumin
1 teaspoon ground turmeric
1 teaspoon garam masala
1 cup (250ml) water
2 tablespoons chopped
fresh coriander

1. Place chickpeas in bowl, cover well with water, cover, stand overnight. Drain chickpeas, add to pan of boiling water, simmer, uncovered, about 45 minutes or until just tender; drain, rinse under cold water, drain.

2. Heat ghee in pan, add onion, galangal and chillies, cook, stirring, until onion is soft. Add chickpeas, combined cumin, turmeric, garam masala and water, simmer, uncovered, about 30 minutes, stirring occasionally, or until liquid is evaporated. Sprinkle with coriander before serving.

Serves 4 to 6.

- Chickpeas best prepared a day ahead.
- Storage: Covered, at room temperature.
- Freeze: Not suitable.
- Microwave: Not suitable.

SQUID AND MARINATED VEGETABLE SALAD

SOTONG DAN SAYUR ASIN

8 medium (1kg) cleaned squid tubes
2 small fresh red chillies,
   seeded, chopped
1 tablespoon chopped fresh
   lemon grass
1 tablespoon grated fresh ginger
1 clove garlic, crushed
1 tablespoon honey
¼ cup (60ml) soy sauce
¼ cup (60ml) vegetable oil
2 tablespoons vegetable oil, extra

MARINATED VEGETABLE SALAD
2 medium (240g) carrots
1 medium (600g) daikon radish
125g snow peas
2 large fresh red chillies, seeded
1 small (800g) pineapple,
   finely chopped
1 medium (150g) onion, finely sliced
¾ cup (180ml) rice wine vinegar
¼ cup (55g) caster sugar
1 tablespoon grated fresh ginger
1 small fresh red chilli,
   seeded, chopped
1 tablespoon chopped
   fresh coriander
1 teaspoon lime juice

1. Cut squid in half, score shallow diagonal slashes in criss-cross pattern on inside surface of squid. Cut squid into 2cm x 5cm pieces.

2. Combine squid, chillies, lemon grass, ginger, garlic, honey, sauce and oil in bowl; mix well. Cover, refrigerate 1 hour.

3. Drain squid from marinade, discard marinade. Heat extra oil in pan, add squid in batches, cook briefly over high heat until tender. Serve squid warm or cold with marinated vegetable salad.

4. Marinated Vegetable Salad: Cut carrots, radish, snow peas and large chillies into thin strips, place in bowl, add pineapple and onion. Pour over combined remaining ingredients; mix well, stand 10 minutes before serving.

Serves 6.

- Recipe can be made 3 hours ahead.
- Storage: Covered, in refrigerator.
- Freeze: Not suitable.
- Microwave: Not suitable.

POTATOES AND SPINACH

UBI KENTANG DAN SAYUR

40g ghee
2 teaspoons finely grated fresh ginger
1 teaspoon ground turmeric
1 teaspoon garam masala
1 teaspoon chilli powder
4 medium (800g) potatoes, chopped
1 cup (250ml) water
1 bunch (650g) English spinach

2. Add water, simmer, covered, about 15 minutes or until potatoes are tender.

3. Stir in spinach leaves, cook, covered, further 2 minutes.

Serves 4.

- Recipe best made just before serving.
- Freeze: Not suitable.
- Microwave: Suitable.

1. Heat ghee in pan, add ginger, turmeric, garam masala and chilli powder, cook, stirring, until fragrant. Add potatoes, cook, stirring, 1 minute.

SPICED YELLOW PUMPKIN

SAGOO

20g ghee
¼ cup (50g) red lentils
1 teaspoon black mustard seeds
5 dried curry leaves
2 cloves garlic, crushed
2 teaspoons ground coriander
1 teaspoon ground cumin
½ teaspoon ground turmeric
3 green shallots, chopped
600g butternut pumpkin,
    peeled, chopped
2 cups (500ml) water
¼ cup (15g) shredded coconut

1. Heat ghee in pan, add lentils, seeds and curry leaves, cook, stirring, until lentils are browned and seeds pop. Add garlic, spices and shallots, cook, stirring, until spices are fragrant.

2. Add pumpkin and water, simmer, covered, 10 minutes. Add coconut, cook, uncovered, further 5 minutes or until pumpkin is tender.

Serves 4.
▦ Recipe best prepared just
    before serving.
▦ Freeze: Not suitable.
▦ Microwave: Suitable.

*Basket and platter from Corso de Fiori; fabric from
Community Aid Abroad Shop.*

PICKLED VEGETABLES

ACAR

Acar is eaten as an appetiser with rice and rendang, or any curry.

1 medium (120g) carrot
150g green beans
½ medium (100g) red pepper
1 small (300g) green cucumber
⅓ cup (50g) roasted
   unsalted peanuts
2 tablespoons vegetable oil
¼ small (300g) cauliflower, chopped
5 leaves Chinese cabbage, shredded
1 cup (250ml) white vinegar
⅓ cup (75g) sugar
½ cup (125ml) water
2 tablespoons toasted sesame seeds

SPICE PASTE
1 teaspoon belacan
1 medium (150g) onion, chopped
2 small fresh red chillies, chopped
1 tablespoon chopped fresh
   lemon grass
4cm piece (70g) fresh galangal,
   chopped
4cm piece (50g) fresh turmeric,
   chopped
3 cloves garlic

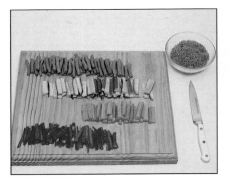

1. Cut carrot, beans, pepper and cucumber into 4cm sticks. Process peanuts until finely minced.

2. Heat oil in pan, add spice paste, cook, stirring, over low heat 10 minutes.

3. Add all the vegetables, vinegar, sugar and water to pan, simmer, uncovered, about 5 minutes or until vegetables are just tender; add peanuts and seeds; cool.

4. Spice Paste: Add belacan to dry pan, cook until dry and crumbly. Blend or process all ingredients until smooth.

MANGO SAMBAL

ACAR MANGGA

1 teaspoon belacan
1 large (600g) mango, peeled
1 small fresh red chilli, finely chopped
1 teaspoon sugar
½ teaspoon soy sauce

2. Cut mango into 1cm cubes. Combine belacan, mango, chilli, sugar and sauce in bowl; mix well.

Serves 4 to 6.

■ Recipe can be made a day ahead.
■ Storage: Covered, in refrigerator.
■ Freeze: Not suitable.
■ Microwave: Not suitable.

1. Add belacan to dry pan, cook until dry and crumbly.

Dish from Community Aid Abroad Shop; basket from Corso de Fiori.

Makes about 1.5 litres (6 cups).

■ Recipe can be made 3 days ahead.
■ Storage: Covered, in refrigerator.
■ Freeze: Not suitable.
■ Microwave: Not suitable.

EGGPLANT AND SHRIMP PASTE SAMBAL

SAMBAL TERUNG

⅓ cup (40g) dried shrimps
1 medium (150g) onion, chopped
2 green shallots, chopped
2 cloves garlic, crushed
2 teaspoons chilli powder
2 teaspoons white vinegar
2 teaspoons sugar
¼ cup (60ml) water
1 tablespoon vegetable oil
2 teaspoons sesame oil
2 medium (600g) eggplants
vegetable oil for deep-frying

1. Place shrimps in heatproof bowl of boiling water for about 10 minutes or until soft; drain. Blend or process shrimps, onion, shallots, garlic, chilli, vinegar, sugar and water until finely chopped.

2. Heat vegetable oil and sesame oil in pan, add shrimp mixture, cook, stirring, about 2 minutes or until fragrant.

3. Cut eggplants into 1cm thick slices. Deep-fry eggplants in batches in hot oil until lightly browned, drain on absorbent paper. Top warm eggplant slices with shrimp mixture.

Serves 6 to 8.

■ Recipe best made just before serving.
■ Freeze: Not suitable.
■ Microwave: Not suitable.

Tray from Corso de Fiori.

GREEN CHILLI SAMBAL

SAMBAL CABAI HIJAU

300g medium fresh green chillies
1 large (200g) onion, chopped
2 candlenuts, chopped
40g ghee
1 tablespoon dried anchovies
½ cup (125ml) coconut milk

1. Cut chillies into 1.5cm lengths.

2. Blend or process onion and candle-nuts until smooth.

3. Heat ghee in pan or wok, add anchovies, cook, stirring, until crisp; drain on absorbent paper. Crumble anchovies. Add onion mixture to pan, stir-fry until onion is soft; add chillies and coconut milk, cook, stirring, about 5 minutes or until chillies are softened slightly. Stir in anchovies; mix well.

Serves 4 to 6.

- Recipe can be made a day ahead.
- Storage: Covered, in refrigerator.
- Freeze: Not suitable.
- Microwave: Not suitable.

ANCHOVY SAMBAL

SAMBAL IKAN BILIS

¼ cup (60ml) vegetable oil
1 cup (90g) firmly packed dried
  anchovies
1 small (80g) onion, sliced
1 teaspoon tamarind concentrate
1 cup (250ml) boiling water
1 tablespoon chopped fresh chives

SEASONING PASTE
8 dried red chillies
2 cloves garlic, halved
4 French shallots, halved
1 teaspoon ground turmeric
1 teaspoon belacan
1 tablespoon grated fresh ginger
1 teaspoon sugar

1. Heat half the oil in pan or wok, add anchovies, cook, stirring, until crisp, remove from pan.

2. Heat remaining oil in pan, add onion, cook, stirring, until soft. Add seasoning paste, cook, stirring, until fragrant. Add combined tamarind concentrate and water, and anchovies, cook over low heat about 20 minutes or until sauce is thickened slightly. Serve sambal topped with chives.

3. Seasoning Paste: Blend or process all ingredients until finely chopped.

Serves 6.
- Recipe can be made a day ahead.
- Storage: Covered, in refrigerator.
- Freeze: Not suitable.
- Microwave: Not suitable.

Box, dish, goblet and cloth from Community Aid Abroad Shop.

PRAWN SAMBAL

SAMBAL UDANG GORENG

2 green shallots
20g ghee
2 teaspoons tamarind paste
1 tablespoon hot water
1 tablespoon grated fresh galangal
2 small fresh green chillies, chopped
2 cloves garlic, crushed
2 teaspoons chopped fresh
   lemon grass
2 dried kaffir lime leaves
1 teaspoon belacan
½ teaspoon ground turmeric
500g medium uncooked
   prawns, shelled
1 cup (250ml) coconut cream

1. Cut shallots into 5cm lengths, cut into strips. Heat 1 teaspoon of the ghee in pan, add shallots, cook, stirring, until browned; drain on absorbent paper. Place tamarind and hot water in bowl; stand 10 minutes. Squeeze liquid from tamarind, strain and reserve liquid; discard tamarind.

2. Heat remaining ghee in pan, add galangal, chillies, garlic, lemon grass, leaves, belacan, turmeric and prawns, cook, stirring, until prawns change colour. Add reserved tamarind liquid and coconut cream, cook, stirring, 2 minutes. Discard leaves, serve topped with shallots.

Serves 4.

■ Recipe best made close to serving.
■ Freeze: Not suitable.
■ Microwave: Not suitable.

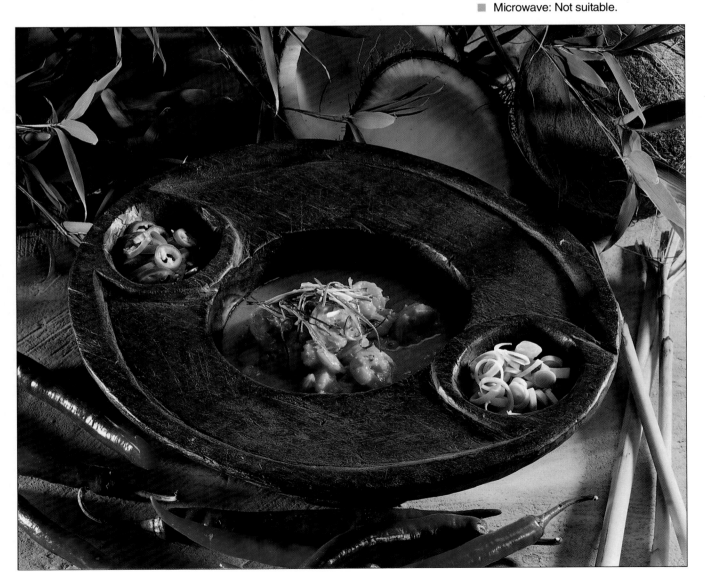

CUCUMBER AND PINEAPPLE SAMBAL

SAMBAL TIMUN DAN NANAS

3 teaspoons belacan
2 small fresh red chillies, seeded,
**   finely chopped**
1 tablespoon lime juice
1 tablespoon soy sauce
1 teaspoon sugar
1 small (130g) green cucumber,
**   peeled, seeded, chopped**
1 small (800g) pineapple, chopped
6 green shallots, sliced

1. Add belacan to dry pan, cook until dry and crumbly. Combine belacan and chillies in small bowl, grind together with mortar and pestle, stir in juice, sauce and sugar; mix well.

2. Combine cucumber, pineapple and shallots in bowl, stir in belacan mixture.

Serves 4 to 6.

■ Recipe can be made a day ahead.
■ Storage: Covered, in refrigerator.
■ Freeze: Not suitable.
■ Microwave: Not suitable.

SHRIMP PASTE SAMBAL

SAMBAL BELACAN

2 tablespoons belacan
8 small fresh red chillies,
**   seeded, chopped**
2 teaspoons lime juice

1. Add belacan to dry pan, cook until dry and crumbly.

2. Pound belacan and chillies in mortar and pestle to a coarse paste, stir in juice.

Makes about 2 tablespoons.

■ Recipe can be made a week ahead.
■ Storage: Covered, in refrigerator.
■ Freeze: Not suitable.
■ Microwave: Not suitable.

Above: Tray from Community Aid Abroad Shop;
dish from Corso de Fiori. Right: Basket from
Corso de Fiori.

Seafood

MAKANAN LAUT

Malaysia lies on a shallow continental shelf surrounded by waters rich in seafood. Over the centuries Malaysians have made the most of this bounty, learning to prepare unusual and delicious recipes using aromatic herbs, spices, pastes and sauces including belacan, tamarind, lemon grass, ginger, coconut milk and chillies. The many and varied combinations of these ingredients produce an endless array of dishes.

PRAWNS WITH BROAD BEANS

UDANG MASAK DENGAN KACANG KACANG

3 small fresh red chillies, chopped
1 tablespoon grated fresh galangal
3 stems fresh lemon grass, chopped
6 green shallots, chopped
2 cloves garlic, crushed
1 teaspoon belacan
750g medium uncooked prawns
1 tablespoon tamarind paste
½ cup (125ml) hot water
80g ghee
2 cups (300g) frozen broad beans, thawed

1. Blend or process chillies, galangal, lemon grass, shallots, garlic and belacan until finely chopped.

2. Shell and devein prawns. Place tamarind and hot water in bowl, stand 10 minutes. Squeeze liquid from tamarind, strain and reserve liquid; discard tamarind.

3. Heat ghee in pan or wok, add chilli mixture, cook, stirring, until fragrant. Add prawns and beans, cook, stirring, until prawns are just cooked; add reserved tamarind liquid, simmer, uncovered, about 2 minutes or until beans are tender.
Serves 4 to 6.

■ Recipe best made just before serving.
■ Freeze: Not suitable.
■ Microwave: Not suitable.

Setting from Morris Home & Garden Wares.

MUSSELS WITH GINGER, GARLIC AND CHILLIES

KERANG TUMIS DENGAN CILI

600g small mussels
2 tablespoons vegetable oil
6 green shallots, chopped
1 tablespoon grated fresh ginger
3 cloves garlic, crushed
2 small fresh red chillies,
   finely chopped
1 teaspoon white soy bean paste
½ teaspoon sugar

3. Add mussels, simmer, covered, about 3 minutes or until mussels are open.

1. Scrub mussels, remove beards. Soak mussels in cold water 15 minutes; drain.

4. Using a slotted spoon, remove mussels from pan. Add sugar to pan, simmer 1 minute. Serve sauce over mussels.

Serves 4.

▧ Recipe best made just before serving.
▧ Freeze: Not suitable.
▧ Microwave: Not suitable.

2. Heat oil in pan, add shallots, ginger, garlic and chillies, cook, stirring, 1 minute. Add soy bean paste, stir until dissolved.

TUNA WITH ONIONS AND STAR FRUIT

SAMBAL IKAN TONGKOL

4 (600g) tuna steaks
½ teaspoon ground turmeric
20g belacan
2 teaspoons tamarind paste
1 tablespoon hot water
1 tablespoon vegetable oil
2 medium (300g) onions, sliced
3 cloves garlic, crushed
1½ teaspoons grated fresh galangal
2 small fresh red chillies,
    seeded, chopped
1 tablespoon soy sauce
1 cup (250ml) water, extra
2 medium (300g) star fruit, sliced

3. Add star fruit, cook, covered, 30 minutes, remove cover, cook, uncovered, further 15 minutes or until fish and star fruit are tender.

Serves 4.

■ Recipe best made just before serving.
■ Freeze: Not suitable.
■ Microwave: Not suitable.

1. Sprinkle fish with turmeric. Add belacan to dry pan, cook, stirring, until dry and crumbly. Place tamarind and hot water in bowl, stand 10 minutes. Squeeze liquid from tamarind, strain and reserve liquid; discard tamarind.

2. Heat oil in pan, add onions and garlic, cook, stirring, until onions are soft. Add belacan, galangal and chillies, cook, stirring, 2 minutes. Add fish, combined reserved tamarind liquid, soy sauce and extra water, bring to boil.

Spice box and tablecloth from Morris Home & Garden Wares.

CHILLI CUTTLEFISH

SOTONG PEDAS

5 (500g) cuttlefish
⅓ cup (80ml) vegetable oil
3 medium (450g) onions, sliced
1 teaspoon sugar
2 teaspoons lime juice

CHILLI PASTE
10 small fresh red chillies,
    seeded, chopped
1 teaspoon belacan

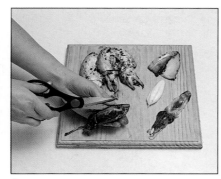

1. To prepare cuttlefish, hold in 1 hand with tentacles facing towards you. Cut along 1 side of "bone" to top of cuttlefish, open out and remove "bone". Gently pull head and tentacles from body. If ink sac is broken, rinse under cold water.

2. Firmly pull skin away, first dipping fingertips into cooking salt. This will help you grip the cuttlefish more easily; wash cuttlefish well. Cut cuttlefish in half lengthways, score shallow diagonal slashes in criss-cross pattern on inside surface of halves.

3. Heat half the oil in pan, add cuttlefish in batches, cook, stirring, about 3 minutes or until tender; remove from pan.

4. Add remaining oil to same pan, add onions, cook, stirring, until soft. Stir in chilli paste, cook, stirring, 1 minute. Stir in sugar and juice, cook, stirring, 1 minute. Return cuttlefish to onion mixture in pan, cook, stirring, until heated through.

5. Chilli Paste: Pound chillies and belacan using a mortar and pestle.

Serves 4.

■ Recipe best made just before serving.
■ Freeze: Not suitable.
■ Microwave: Not suitable.

Plate and bowls from Accoutrement.

FISH IN RENDANG SAUCE

RENDANG IKAN

750g blue-eyed cod fillets
2 tablespoons lime juice
½ teaspoon sugar
1½ tablespoons tamarind paste
¼ cup (60ml) hot water
2 tablespoons vegetable oil
1½ cups (375ml) coconut milk
⅓ cup (30g) coconut, toasted

CHILLI PASTE
2 medium (300g) onions, chopped
4 cloves garlic, crushed
3 small fresh red chillies,
**   seeded, chopped**
1 tablespoon chopped fresh
**   lemon grass**
3 teaspoons grated fresh galangal
1 tablespoon grated fresh ginger
1 teaspoon belacan
2 fresh kaffir lime leaves
½ teaspoon ground turmeric
2 teaspoons mild curry powder

1. Cut fish into 3cm cubes. Combine fish, juice and sugar in bowl; cover, stand 1 hour. Place tamarind and hot water in bowl, stand 10 minutes. Squeeze liquid from tamarind, strain and reserve liquid, discard tamarind.

2. Heat oil in pan, add chilli paste, cook, stirring, until fragrant. Gradually stir in reserved tamarind liquid, coconut milk, and half the coconut.

3. Add fish to pan, simmer, uncovered, about 10 minutes or until fish is cooked and sauce is thickened slightly. Sprinkle with remaining coconut.

4. Chilli Paste: Blend or process all ingredients until well combined.

Serves 4.

- Recipe best made on day of serving.
- Storage: Covered, in refrigerator.
- Freeze: Not suitable.
- Microwave: Not suitable.

CUTTLEFISH WITH PRAWNS AND PEANUT SAUCE

SAMBAL SOTONG DAN UDANG

12 (1.2kg) cuttlefish
500g uncooked prawns, shelled, chopped
1 tablespoon chopped fresh parsley
2 teaspoons tamarind paste
1 tablespoon hot water
1 cup (150g) peanuts, roasted
4 small fresh red chillies, chopped
10 green shallots, chopped
1 stem fresh lemon grass, chopped
1 tablespoon grated fresh ginger
2 cloves garlic, crushed
60g ghee
1½ cups (375ml) coconut milk
1 tablespoon palm sugar

1. To prepare cuttlefish, hold in 1 hand with tentacles facing towards you. Cut along 1 side of "bone" to top of cuttlefish, open out and remove "bone". Gently pull head and tentacles from body. If ink sac is broken, rinse under cold water.

2. Firmly pull skin away, first dipping fingertips into cooking salt. This will help you grip the cuttlefish more easily; wash cuttlefish well.

3. Combine prawns and parsley in bowl, mix well.

4. Roll each cuttlefish to form a cone shape, secure with toothpicks. Spoon a tablespoon of prawn mixture into each cuttlefish cavity; press firmly.

5. Place tamarind and hot water in bowl, stand 10 minutes. Squeeze liquid from tamarind, strain and reserve liquid, discard tamarind. Blend or process peanuts, chillies, shallots, lemon grass, ginger and garlic until finely chopped.

6. Heat ghee in wok or pan, add peanut mixture, cook, stirring, until fragrant. Add reserved tamarind liquid, coconut milk and sugar, bring to boil; add cuttlefish; simmer, covered, about 10 minutes, stirring occasionally, or until cooked through.

Serves 4.

■ Recipe best made just before serving.
■ Freeze: Not suitable.
■ Microwave: Not suitable.

Copper bowl, jug and candlesticks from Parkers of Turramurra; fabric from Morris Home & Garden Wares.

FISH WITH BLACK BEAN SAUCE

IKAN GORENG MASAK TAUCHEO

½ cup (80g) packaged salted
    black beans
⅓ cup (80ml) water
1 tablespoon soy sauce
1 tablespoon sugar
1 teaspoon sesame oil
1 teaspoon cornflour
1 tablespoon white vinegar
4 x 450g whole snapper
¼ cup (60ml) vegetable oil
1 tablespoon vegetable oil, extra
1 tablespoon finely grated
    fresh ginger
4 cloves garlic, crushed
500ml fish stock
2 small fresh red chillies,
    finely chopped
6 green shallots, chopped

1. Blend or process beans and water to form a paste. Combine soy sauce, sugar, sesame oil and blended cornflour and vinegar in bowl; mix well.

2. Score fish 3 times on each side. Heat vegetable oil in pan until very hot, add fish in batches, cook until crisp and browned on both sides; drain on absorbent paper. Transfer fish to baking dish.

3. Heat extra vegetable oil in pan, add bean mixture, ginger and garlic, cook, stirring, until fragrant. Add soy sauce mixture and stock, cook, stirring, until slightly thickened. Stir in chillies and shallots, simmer, uncovered, 2 minutes. Pour mixture over fish, simmer, uncovered, on stove top about 5 minutes or until fish are tender.

Serves 4.

■ Recipe best made just before serving.
■ Freeze: Not suitable.
■ Microwave: Not suitable.

Setting from Morris Home & Garden Wares.

SWEET SOUR FISH

IKAN ASSAM-MANIS

1 small (130g) green cucumber
2 medium (260g) tomatoes, peeled
1 large (200g) onion
1 tablespoon ghee
2 cloves garlic, crushed
2 small fresh red chillies, chopped
1 teaspoon grated fresh galangal
2 cups (500ml) water
2 tablespoons tomato sauce
2 tablespoons plum sauce
1 tablespoon mild sweet chilli sauce
2 teaspoons white vinegar
1 tablespoon sugar
1 tablespoon cornflour
1 tablespoon water, extra
6 (860g) boneless firm white
    fish fillets
cornflour, extra
vegetable oil for deep-frying

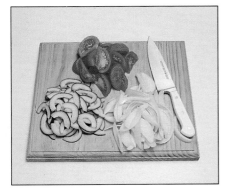

1. Cut cucumber in half lengthways, scoop out seeds; slice cucumber. Cut tomatoes and onion into wedges.

2. Heat ghee in pan, add onion, garlic, chillies and galangal, cook, stirring, until onion is soft. Add water, sauces, vinegar and sugar, simmer, uncovered, 5 minutes. Stir in cucumber, tomatoes, and blended cornflour and extra water; stir over heat until sauce boils and thickens.

3. Toss fish in extra cornflour, shake away excess flour. Deep-fry fish in batches in hot oil until browned and cooked through; drain on absorbent paper. Serve fish with sauce.

Serves 6.
■ Recipe best made just before serving.
■ Freeze: Not suitable.
■ Microwave: Not suitable.

DRY SQUID CURRY

OPOR SOTONG

500g squid tubes
2 tablespoons mild chilli powder
1 teaspoon ground turmeric
1 tablespoon tamarind paste
2 tablespoons hot water
2 tablespoons vegetable oil
2 medium (300g) onions,
   finely chopped
4 cloves garlic, crushed
2 tablespoons tomato sauce
1 teaspoon soy sauce
1 tablespoon fish sauce
½ teaspoon sugar
⅓ cup (80ml) lemon juice
2 tablespoons packaged fried onions

1. Cut squid into rings. Combine squid, chilli powder and turmeric in bowl; mix well. Place tamarind paste and hot water in bowl, stand 10 minutes. Squeeze liquid from tamarind, strain and reserve liquid; discard tamarind.

2. Heat oil in pan, add squid mixture, cook, stirring, until squid changes colour; remove from pan.

3. Add onions and garlic to same pan, cook, stirring, until onions are soft. Add reserved tamarind liquid, sauces and sugar, cook, stirring occasionally, about 4 minutes.

4. Return squid to pan, add juice, stir over heat until squid is tender. Serve curry sprinkled with fried onions.

Serves 4.

- Recipe can be made a day ahead.
- Storage: Covered, in refrigerator.
- Freeze: Not suitable.
- Microwave: Not suitable.

PRAWN AND EGGPLANT CURRY

KARI UDANG DAN TERUNG

600g uncooked medium prawns
8 French shallots, halved
1 teaspoon chilli powder
1 teaspoon ground turmeric
1 teaspoon belacan
1 teaspoon sugar
50g ghee
2 medium (300g) onions, sliced
2 cups (500ml) coconut milk
1 cup (250ml) water
8 (480g) finger eggplants, chopped
4 dried curry leaves

1. Shell and devein prawns, leaving tails intact. Blend or process shallots, chilli, turmeric, belacan and sugar until shallots are finely chopped.

2. Heat ghee in wok or pan, add onions, cook, stirring, until soft. Add shallot mixture, cook, stirring, until fragrant. Add coconut milk and water, simmer, uncovered, 10 minutes.

3. Add eggplants and curry leaves to coconut mixture, cook, uncovered, about 15 minutes or until eggplants are tender. Stir in prawns, cook, uncovered, until prawns are tender. Discard curry leaves before serving.

Serves 4.

- Blended mixture can be prepared 3 days ahead.
- Storage: Covered, in refrigerator.
- Freeze: Not suitable.
- Microwave: Not suitable.

CHILLI CRAB

CILI KETAM

2 x 1.25kg uncooked mud crabs
2 teaspoons belacan
6 cloves garlic, crushed
1 tablespoon grated fresh ginger
2 tablespoons soy sauce
½ cup (125ml) tomato sauce
3 teaspoons sambal oelek
2 tablespoons rice wine vinegar
2 teaspoons brown sugar
1 tablespoon vegetable oil
1 tablespoon cornflour
½ cup (125ml) water

1. Place live crabs in freezer at least 2 hours; this is the most humane way of killing a crab. Slide a sharp strong knife under top of shell at back of crab, lever off shell and discard.

2. Remove and discard gills, wash crab thoroughly. Chop body into quarters with cleaver, remove claws and nippers, chop nippers into large pieces.

3. Add belacan to dry pan, cook until dry and crumbly. Combine belacan, garlic, ginger, sauces, sambal oelek, vinegar and sugar in bowl; mix well.

4. Heat oil in large pan, add chilli mixture and crab, cook, covered, about 10 minutes or until crab is cooked through.

5. Remove crab from pan, place on serving dish. Stir blended cornflour and water into chilli mixture in pan, stir over heat until mixture boils and thickens slightly. Pour chilli sauce over crab.

Serves 4.

■ Recipe best made just before serving.
■ Freeze: Not suitable.
■ Microwave: Not suitable.

TAMARIND FISH WITH EGGPLANT

IKAN ASSAM DAN TERUNG

1 tablespoon chopped fresh
  lemon grass
1 tablespoon grated fresh galangal
2 teaspoons belacan
8 French shallots, halved
2 teaspoons sambal oelek
8 candlenuts
50g ghee
2 medium (300g) onions, thinly sliced
1 teaspoon tamarind concentrate
2½ cups (625ml) water
8 (480g) finger eggplants, sliced
750g trevally fillets, sliced
3 medium (390g) tomatoes,
  seeded, chopped

1. Blend or process lemon grass, galangal, belacan, shallots, sambal oelek and candlenuts until finely chopped.

2. Heat ghee in wok or pan, add onions, cook, stirring, until soft. Add lemon grass mixture, cook, stirring, until fragrant. Stir in combined tamarind concentrate and water, simmer, uncovered, 10 minutes.

3. Add eggplants, simmer, covered, about 15 minutes or until tender.

4. Stir in fish and tomatoes, cook, covered, about 10 minutes or until fish is cooked through.

Serves 4.

- Lemon grass mixture can be prepared 3 days ahead.
- Storage: Covered, in refrigerator.
- Freeze: Blended mixture suitable.
- Microwave: Not suitable.

Poultry

MAKANAN DAGING AYAM

Chicken is the most popular meat after seafood in Malaysia and it is prepared in many ways – marinated and grilled, fried or cooked in aromatic curries and sauces. Dishes reflect the main ethnic groups within the country; piquant Indian spices combine with Chinese herbs to produce a Malay taste sensation. Try our recipes for a delectable and different chicken main course, served with a bowl of steaming rice and accompaniments of your choice.

DRY CHICKEN CURRY

OPOR AYAM

¼ cup (60ml) vegetable oil
8 chicken thigh cutlets
4 medium (600g) onions, sliced
2 tablespoons grated fresh ginger
1 cinnamon stick
2 teaspoons chilli powder
2 teaspoons ground cumin
2 teaspoons ground coriander
2 tablespoons lime juice

1. Heat half the oil in pan, add chicken in batches, cook, turning, until well browned; drain on absorbent paper.

2. Heat remaining oil in same pan, add onions, ginger, cinnamon, chilli and spices, cook, stirring, until onions are soft. Return chicken to pan, add juice, cook, covered, about 15 minutes or until chicken is tender. Remove and discard cinnamon before serving.

Serves 4.

■ Recipe can be made a day ahead.
■ Storage: Covered, in refrigerator.
■ Freeze: Suitable.
■ Microwave: Not suitable.

CHICKEN SATAY

SATAY AYAM

1kg chicken thigh fillets
1 teaspoon ground coriander
1 teaspoon ground cumin
½ teaspoon ground cinnamon
2 teaspoons grated fresh turmeric
¼ cup (35g) roasted peanuts,
    finely chopped
1 teaspoon sugar
2 cloves garlic, crushed
3 teaspoons vegetable oil
1 teaspoon sesame oil
1 teaspoon mild sweet chilli sauce

PEANUT SAUCE
2 cups (300g) roasted peanuts
1 tablespoon grated fresh ginger
4 cloves garlic, crushed
1 tablespoon grated fresh galangal
2 small fresh red chillies, chopped
⅓ cup chopped fresh lemon grass
2 tablespoons tamarind paste
2 tablespoons hot water
2 tablespoons vegetable oil
1 large (200g) onion, chopped
2 tablespoons palm sugar
1 cup (250ml) water, extra

1. Cut chicken into 2cm pieces. Combine chicken and remaining ingredients in bowl; mix well. Cover, refrigerate several hours or overnight.

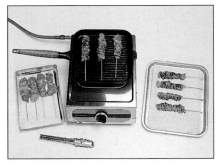

2. Thread chicken onto 16 skewers. Heat griddle pan, add chicken in batches, cook until well browned and cooked through. Serve with peanut sauce.

3. Peanut Sauce: Blend or process peanuts until fine. Blend or process ginger, garlic, galangal, chillies and lemon grass until well combined. Place tamarind and hot water in bowl, stand 10 minutes. Squeeze liquid from tamarind, strain and reserve liquid; discard tamarind.

4. Heat oil in pan, add onion, cook, stirring, until onion is soft. Add peanuts, lemon grass mixture, reserved tamarind liquid, sugar and extra water, simmer, uncovered, until thickened slightly.

Serves 4.

- Chicken and peanut sauce can be made a day ahead.
- Storage: Covered, separately, in refrigerator.
- Freeze: Uncooked marinated chicken suitable.
- Microwave: Not suitable.

CHICKEN IN TOMATO COCONUT SAUCE

GULAI AYAM LEMAK

8 chicken drumsticks
½ teaspoon ground turmeric
2 tablespoons vegetable oil
8 green shallots, chopped
2 cloves garlic, crushed
2 tablespoons grated fresh ginger
8 dried red chillies, chopped
1 tablespoon vegetable oil, extra
5 cloves
1 star anise
2 cups (500ml) coconut milk
425g can tomato puree
1 cinnamon stick
1 large (200g) onion, sliced
1 large (250g) tomato, sliced
1 cup (125g) frozen peas

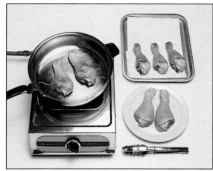

1. Using plastic gloves to prevent staining hands, rub chicken with turmeric. Heat oil in pan, add chicken in batches, cook until browned; drain on absorbent paper.

2. Blend or process shallots, garlic, ginger and chillies until finely chopped.

3. Heat extra oil in pan, add shallot mixture, cloves and star anise, cook, stirring, 1 minute. Add coconut milk, simmer, uncovered, 2 minutes.

4. Add chicken, tomato puree and cinnamon, simmer, uncovered, about 10 minutes or until chicken is tender. Stir in onion, tomato and peas, cook, uncovered, about 3 minutes or until peas are tender. Remove cinnamon before serving.

Serves 4.

- Recipe can be made a day ahead.
- Storage: Covered, in refrigerator.
- Freeze: Suitable.
- Microwave: Not suitable.

CURRY KAPITAN WITH ROTI JALA

KARI KAPITAN DAN ROTI JALA

2 tablespoons vegetable oil
2 medium (300g) onions, sliced
¼ cup (60ml) water
1.5kg chicken pieces
2 x 270ml cans coconut milk
1 cup (250ml) coconut cream

SPICE PASTE
10 small fresh red chillies
4 cloves garlic
3 teaspoons grated fresh turmeric
2 teaspoons grated fresh galangal
2 teaspoons chopped fresh
    lemon grass
10 candlenuts
1 tablespoon ground cumin

ROTI JALA
1 cup (150g) plain flour
1½ cups (375ml) milk
1 egg

1. Heat oil in pan, add onions, cook, stirring, until soft. Stir in spice paste and water, cook, stirring, until fragrant.

2. Add chicken and coconut milk, simmer, covered, 20 minutes, remove lid, simmer, uncovered, further 20 minutes, stirring occasionally, or until chicken is tender. Stir in coconut cream, serve with roti jala.

3. Spice Paste: Blend or process all ingredients until smooth.

4. Roti Jala: Sift flour into bowl, gradually stir in combined milk and egg, beat until smooth. Strain batter into jug to remove lumps and make pouring easier.

5. Heat greased 24cm pan over medium heat. Pour about ¼ cup (60ml) of batter from jug into pan, moving jug back and forth so that pancake will have a lacy appearance. Cook until lightly browned underneath and cooked on top, transfer to greaseproof paper, stand 1 minute, fold in half and in half again to form a triangle. Repeat with remaining batter.

Serves 4 to 6.

■ Chicken curry and roti jala can be prepared a day ahead.
■ Storage: Covered, in refrigerator.
■ Freeze: Not suitable.
■ Microwave: Not suitable.

Plates from Ventura Imports.

CHICKEN IN COCONUT SAUCE

AYAM MASAK LEMAK

8 candlenuts
4 cloves garlic, halved
4 French shallots, halved
1 tablespoon grated fresh ginger
1 tablespoon grated fresh galangal
1 tablespoon chopped fresh
   lemon grass
1 tablespoon grated fresh turmeric
1 teaspoon sambal oelek
50g ghee
1.6kg chicken pieces
4 fresh kaffir lime leaves
2 cups (500ml) coconut milk
1 cup (250ml) chicken stock
2 tablespoons packaged fried onions
1 tablespoon chopped fresh chives

1. Blend or process candlenuts, garlic, shallots, ginger, galangal, lemon grass, turmeric and sambal oelek until ingredients are finely chopped.

2. Heat 2 teaspoons of the ghee in pan, add chicken in batches, cook until browned on both sides; drain chicken on absorbent paper, reserve pan.

3. Cut lime leaves into very thin strips. Heat remaining ghee in same pan, add candlenut mixture, cook, stirring, about 5 minutes. Add coconut milk, stock and lime leaves, simmer, uncovered, 5 minutes. Add chicken to coconut mixture, cook, covered, until chicken is tender. Serve sprinkled with fried onions and chives.

Serves 4.

■ Candlenut paste can be made a day ahead.
■ Storage: Covered, in refrigerator.
■ Freeze: Not suitable.
■ Microwave: Not suitable.

SPICY FRIED CHICKEN

AYAM GORENG PEDAS

2 cloves garlic, crushed
1 tablespoon grated fresh ginger
1 teaspoon ground cinnamon
½ teaspoon ground nutmeg
½ teaspoon cracked black pepper
8 (1kg) chicken thigh cutlets
20g ghee
1 cup (130g) unroasted cashews
3 small fresh green chillies, chopped
½ cup (125ml) water
½ small (500g) cauliflower, chopped
½ cup (60g) frozen peas, thawed
2 medium (260g) tomatoes, chopped
2 hard-boiled eggs, halved

1. Combine garlic, ginger, cinnamon, nutmeg and pepper in bowl; mix well. Rub garlic mixture over chicken, cover, refrigerate 1 hour.

2. Heat ghee in heavy-based pan, add chicken in batches, cook, turning occasionally, until well browned all over; drain on absorbent paper.

3. Blend or process nuts until finely chopped. Return chicken to pan, add nuts and chillies, cook, stirring, 1 minute. Add water and cauliflower, simmer, covered, about 15 minutes or until chicken is tender.

4. Add peas and tomatoes, cook, stirring gently, until peas are just soft. Just before serving, top with eggs.

Serves 4.

- Recipe can be made a day ahead.
- Storage: Covered, in refrigerator.
- Freeze: Not suitable.
- Microwave: Not suitable.

Bowl and cane tray from Zuhause.

CRISPY FRIED CHICKEN

AYAM GORENG

1.5kg chicken
2 teaspoons salt
¼ teaspoon five spice powder
1 cinnamon stick
6 star anise
2cm (40g) piece fresh galangal
1 lime, chopped
2.75 litres (11 cups) vegetable oil for deep-frying

GLAZE
1 tablespoon honey
2 teaspoons soy sauce
1 teaspoon ground coriander
1 teaspoon garam masala
½ teaspoon chilli powder
½ teaspoon ground cinnamon

1. Remove fat from inside chicken, pat dry with absorbent paper, rub inside with combined salt and five spice powder. Place cinnamon, star anise and galangal inside chicken, secure ends with skewers, tuck wings under.

2. Heat enough water in large pan to cover chicken, add lime, bring to boil. Lower chicken into pan breast side down, holding legs together, cook 2 minutes.

3. Drain chicken; pat dry with absorbent paper. Place chicken, breast side up, on wire rack over oven tray. Brush hot chicken with some of the glaze, stand 10 minutes. Brush again with remaining glaze (glaze may need to be re-heated). Refrigerate chicken overnight uncovered.

4. Next day, heat oil (oil should be about 8cm deep) in wok or large pan. Place chicken in large strainer, carefully lower chicken, breast side up, into oil. A large slotted spoon can also be used; keep spoon under chicken while frying to prevent chicken coming into contact with base of wok. Spoon or ladle hot oil over exposed part of chicken constantly, cook 20 minutes, drain chicken on wire rack 10 minutes. Reheat oil, lower chicken into oil, cook as before, about 10 minutes or until skin puffs up and becomes dark golden brown; drain on absorbent paper.

5. Glaze: Heat all ingredients in pan.

Serves 4.

- ■ Recipe must be prepared a day ahead.
- ■ Storage: Uncovered, in refrigerator.
- ■ Freeze: Not suitable.
- ■ Microwave: Not suitable.

DUCK WITH GINGER AND MUSHROOMS

ITEK MASAK CINA

2.2kg duck
⅓ cup (80ml) soy sauce
6 Chinese dried mushrooms
vegetable oil for deep-frying
1 tablespoon vegetable oil, extra
5cm piece (40g) fresh ginger,
**   thinly sliced**
2 cloves garlic, crushed
1 litre (4 cups) water
1 tablespoon hoi sin sauce
1 teaspoon sugar
2 teaspoons sesame oil
¼ teaspoon ground black pepper
1 tablespoon tapioca flour
1 tablespoon water, extra
1 tablespoon rice wine
2 green shallots, thinly sliced

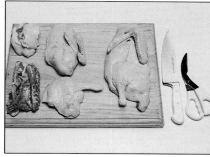

1. Place duck on board, breast side up. Cut through breastbone, a little to 1 side, and right through backbone. Cut both pieces of duck in half; discard excess fat and bone.

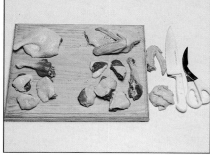

2. Remove first 2 bones of wings, discard; cut each breast into 6 pieces. Cut each thigh and leg into 4 pieces; discard excess fat.

3. Combine duck and 1 tablespoon of the soy sauce in bowl, cover, refrigerate 20 minutes. Place mushrooms in heatproof bowl, cover with boiling water, stand 20 minutes. Drain mushrooms, discard stems, cut caps in half.

4. Deep-fry duck in batches in hot oil until browned; drain on absorbent paper.

5. Heat extra oil in pan, add ginger and garlic, cook, stirring, until lightly browned, add duck, mushrooms, remaining soy sauce, water, hoi sin sauce, sugar, sesame oil and pepper. Boil, uncovered, about 15 minutes or until duck is tender and sauce reduced to about 2 cups (500ml). Add blended tapioca flour and extra water, stir over heat until sauce boils and thickens; stir in wine and shallots.

Serves 4.

■ Recipe can be made a day ahead.
■ Storage: Covered, in refrigerator.
■ Freeze: Not suitable.
■ Microwave: Not suitable.

CHICKEN AND POTATO CURRY

KARI AYAM DAN UBI KENTANG

2.2kg chicken
⅔ cup (80g) mild curry powder
⅔ cup (160ml) water
7 cloves garlic, crushed
5 green shallots, finely chopped
2 teaspoons grated fresh ginger
⅓ cup (80ml) vegetable oil
1 litre (4 cups) coconut milk
3 medium (600g) potatoes, peeled, chopped
2 medium (300g) onions, sliced
5 green shallots, chopped, extra

1. Place chicken on board, breast side up. Cut through breastbone, a little to 1 side, and right through backbone. Cut both pieces of chicken in half.

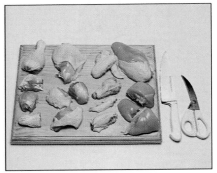

2. Cut between each wing and breast, cutting through joint. Cut or chop between each leg and thigh, making a total of 8 pieces. Chop each wing, leg, breast and thigh into 3 pieces, making 24 pieces.

3. Blend or process curry powder, water, garlic, shallots and ginger until smooth. Combine curry mixture and chicken in bowl, cover, refrigerate 30 minutes.

4. Heat oil in pan, add chicken, cook, stirring, about 10 minutes or until chicken is browned and fragrant.

5. Add coconut milk, potatoes and onions, simmer, uncovered, about 20 minutes or until potatoes are tender. Stir in extra shallots.

Serves 4 to 6.

■ Recipe can be made a day ahead.
■ Storage: Covered, in refrigerator.
■ Freeze: Not suitable.
■ Microwave: Not suitable.

Meat

MAKANAN DAGING LEMBU DAN KAMBING

The wide variety of spicy meat dishes offered in Malaysian cuisine reflect the many ethnic origins of the people. Meat is often marinated in delicious spices while clay and earthenware pots or cast-iron woks are the preferred cookware. Meat dishes are traditionally served with bowls of steaming rice and a selection of side dishes, such as vegetables, sambals and soups, which provide a myriad of taste flavours and textures.

LAMB RAAN

ROS KAMBING

2kg leg of lamb
4 cloves garlic, chopped
1 medium (150g) onion, chopped
1 tablespoon grated fresh ginger
1 teaspoon ground cardamom
½ teaspoon ground cloves
1 tablespoon lemon juice
½ teaspoon sambal oelek
50g ghee
1 medium (150g) onion, finely chopped, extra
1 cup (70g) stale breadcrumbs
½ cup (75g) pistachios, finely chopped
½ cup (60g) packaged ground almonds
1 teaspoon ground turmeric
¼ teaspoon chilli powder

1. Place lamb, fat side down, on board. Cut into lamb, following the length of the bone. Then scrape meat away from bone until bone is exposed and easy to remove; discard bone.

2. Blend or process garlic, onion, ginger, spices, juice and sambal oelek to a smooth paste. Cut 4 x 1cm slits into lamb on both sides. Place lamb in baking dish, rub onion paste into and over lamb, cover, refrigerate overnight.

3. Heat ghee in pan, add extra onion, cook, stirring, until soft. Combine extra onion and remaining ingredients in bowl; mix well. Press breadcrumb mixture over top of lamb.

4. Bake lamb, uncovered, in moderately hot oven about 1¼ hours or until crust is browned and meat tender.

Serves 6.

- Recipe can be prepared a day ahead.
- Storage: Covered, in refrigerator.
- Freeze: Not suitable.
- Microwave: Not suitable.

PORK AND BEEF SATAYS WITH PEANUT SAUCE

SATAY BABI DAN LEMBU DAN KUAH KACANG

Soak bamboo skewers in water for several hours or overnight to prevent them from burning.

500g beef fillet
500g pork fillet
4 cloves garlic, crushed
1 teaspoon ground cumin
1 teaspoon ground coriander
2 teaspoons ground turmeric
2 tablespoons vegetable oil

PEANUT SAUCE
8 green shallots, chopped
1 cup (150g) unsalted roasted
  peanuts
2 teaspoons vegetable oil
1 tablespoon chopped fresh
  lemon grass
1 clove garlic, crushed
1 teaspoon grated fresh ginger
1 teaspoon sambal oelek
1 teaspoon ground cumin
1 teaspoon ground coriander
½ teaspoon ground turmeric
1 cup (250ml) chicken stock
1 cup (250ml) coconut milk
2 teaspoons lemon juice

1. Cut beef and pork into 8cm strips, about 1.5cm thick; thread evenly onto 18 bamboo skewers.

2. Place skewers on oven trays, brush with combined garlic, spices and half the oil; cover, refrigerate 3 hours or overnight.

3. Heat remaining oil in pan, cook skewers in batches until well browned and tender. Serve with peanut sauce.

4. Peanut Sauce: Blend or process shallots and peanuts until finely chopped. Heat oil in pan, add peanut mixture, lemon grass, garlic, ginger and spices, cook, stirring, 2 minutes.

5. Stir in stock and coconut milk, simmer, uncovered, about 5 minutes or until slightly thickened, stir in juice.

Serves 6.

■ Recipe can be prepared a day ahead.
■ Storage: Covered, in refrigerator.
■ Freeze: Uncooked marinated skewers suitable.
■ Microwave: Sauce suitable.

Carving from Java Bazaar.

MUTTON AND POTATO CURRY

KAN KAMBING DAN UBI KENTANG

½ cup firmly packed fresh
   coriander leaves
4 cloves garlic, crushed
6 green shallots, chopped
2 tablespoons grated fresh galangal
2 tablespoons grated fresh ginger
1kg diced mutton
2 tablespoons vegetable oil
2 large (400g) onions, sliced
¼ teaspoon ground cardamom
6 cloves
½ teaspoon ground anise
1 teaspoon ground turmeric
½ teaspoon ground cumin
2 cups (500ml) coconut milk
400g baby new potatoes, halved
2 tablespoons packaged ground
   almonds

1. Blend or process coriander, garlic, shallots, galangal and ginger until well combined. Combine mutton and coriander mixture in bowl; mix well. Cover, refrigerate several hours or overnight.

2. Heat half the oil in flameproof dish, add mutton in batches, cook until well browned all over; remove from pan.

3. Heat remaining oil in same dish, add onions, cook, stirring, until soft. Add cardamom, cloves, anise, turmeric and cumin; cook, stirring, 2 minutes.

4. Return mutton to dish, add coconut milk, simmer, uncovered, 3 minutes, cover with foil. Bake in moderately slow oven 1 hour, add potatoes, bake further 1 hour or until mutton and potatoes are tender. Add nuts, cook, stirring, until heated through.

Serves 4 to 6.

▪ Recipe best made just before serving.
▪ Freeze: Not suitable.
▪ Microwave: Not suitable.

BEEF WITH MUSHROOMS AND EGG NOODLES

MEE GORENG

2 cups (60g) Chinese dried
    mushrooms
2 green shallots, chopped
3 cloves garlic, crushed
1 tablespoon grated fresh ginger
2 small fresh red chillies, chopped
1 teaspoon sesame oil
20g ghee
500g minced beef
1 medium (200g) red pepper, sliced
1 cup (250ml) coconut milk
400g fresh thick egg noodles
2 tablespoons vegetable oil

1. Place mushrooms in heatproof bowl, cover with boiling water, stand 20 minutes. Drain mushrooms; discard stems, chop caps. Blend or process mushrooms, shallots, garlic, ginger and chillies until finely chopped.

2. Heat sesame oil and ghee in pan, add mushroom mixture, cook, stirring,

2 minutes. Add mince, cook, stirring, until well browned. Add pepper and coconut milk, cook, stirring, until pepper is just soft.

3. Add noodles to large pan of boiling water, boil, uncovered, about 3 minutes or until tender; drain. Toss noodles in vegetable oil; serve with mince mixture.

Serves 4.

- Mince mixture can be made a day ahead.
- Storage: Covered, in refrigerator.
- Freeze: Not suitable.
- Microwave: Noodles suitable.

Setting from Accoutrement.

BEEF STIR-FRY WITH GINGER AND SHALLOTS

DAGING LEMBU GORENG CINA

1 clove garlic, crushed
1 tablespoon cornflour
½ teaspoon bicarbonate of soda
1 egg white
500g beef fillet, thinly sliced
6cm piece (50g) fresh ginger,
thinly sliced
coarse cooking salt
10 green shallots
50g ghee
¼ cup (60ml) water
1 tablespoon oyster sauce

ghee in wok or pan until very hot, add shallots and ginger, cook, stirring, over high heat 1 minute, remove from wok.

1. Combine garlic, cornflour, soda and egg white in bowl, add beef; mix well. Cover, refrigerate 30 minutes.

2. Combine ginger and salt in bowl, cover, stand 20 minutes. Rinse ginger under water, drain; pat dry with absorbent paper. Cut shallots into 5cm lengths. Heat

3. Reheat same wok, add beef mixture and water, cook, stirring, over high heat until beef is just tender. Add shallots, ginger and oyster sauce, cook, stirring, until heated through.

Serves 4.

■ Recipe best prepared just before serving.
■ Freeze: Not suitable.
■ Microwave: Not suitable.

Carving from Java Bazaar.

ROLLED PORK NECK WITH LEAFY VEGETABLES

TANYEW BAK DAN SAYUR

1/3 cup (80ml) vegetable oil
1.5kg piece pork neck, rolled, tied
2½ cups (625ml) chicken stock
1 tablespoon oyster sauce
1 teaspoon fish sauce
1 tablespoon soy sauce
1 teaspoon palm sugar
2 bunches (450g) baby bok choy,
    roughly shredded
2 bunches (1.3kg) English spinach,
    roughly shredded

3. Heat remaining oil in clean pan, add vegetables, cook, stirring, until just wilted; drain. Combine vegetables and reserved stock; mix well. Serve pork sliced over leafy vegetables.

Serves 4 to 6.

▪ Pork can be prepared a day ahead. Cook vegetables just before serving.
▪ Storage: Covered, in refrigerator.
▪ Freeze: Not suitable.
▪ Microwave: Not suitable.

1. Heat half the oil in large pan, add pork, cook, turning, until well browned all over. Add stock, simmer, covered, about 1½ hours or until pork is tender.

2. Stir in sauces and sugar, simmer, covered, further 15 minutes. Remove pork, stand 5 minutes, reduce stock to 1 cup (250ml), reserve stock.

BEEF KURMAH

KARI KURMAH

2 tablespoons vegetable oil
1kg chuck steak, sliced
8 green shallots, chopped
2 cloves garlic, crushed
1 tablespoon grated fresh ginger
3 teaspoons ground coriander
1 tablespoon ground cumin
2 teaspoons ground anise
1 cinnamon stick
4 cloves
3 cardamom pods
1 tablespoon chopped fresh
    lemon grass
2 cups (500ml) coconut milk
1 small fresh red chilli, chopped
½ cup (60g) packaged ground
    almonds

3. Return steak to pan, add coconut milk and chilli, simmer, covered, about 1 hour or until steak is tender. Add nuts, stir until heated through. Discard cinnamon and cardamom before serving.

Serves 4.

▓ Recipe can be made a day ahead.
▓ Storage: Covered, in refrigerator.
▓ Freeze: Suitable.
▓ Microwave: Not suitable.

1. Heat half the oil in pan, add steak in batches, cook until browned all over; remove from pan.

2. Heat remaining oil in same pan, add shallots, garlic and ginger, cook, stirring, until shallots are soft. Add coriander, cumin, anise, cinnamon, cloves, cardamom and lemon grass, cook, stirring, 3 minutes.

Plate from Accoutrement; fabric from Java Bazaar.

PORK PATTIES WITH STIR-FRIED VEGETABLES

KABAB BABI DAN SAYUR SAYURAN

600g minced pork
2 teaspoons soy sauce
1 teaspoon sesame oil
2 cloves garlic, crushed
½ teaspoon sambal oelek
½ cup (35g) stale breadcrumbs
1 egg, lightly beaten
50g ghee
2 medium (300g) onions, sliced
2 medium (260g) tomatoes, chopped
200g snow peas
150g bean sprouts
1 tablespoon hoi sin sauce
1 tablespoon fresh coriander leaves

1. Combine mince, soy sauce, oil, garlic, sambal oelek, breadcrumbs and egg in bowl; mix well. Divide mixture into 8 portions, shape into patties.

2. Heat ghee in pan, add patties in batches, cook until browned on both sides and cooked through; drain on absorbent paper.

3. Drain away all but 2 tablespoons of ghee from pan. Reheat ghee, add onions, cook, stirring, until soft. Add tomatoes, snow peas, bean sprouts and hoi sin sauce, cook, stirring, until vegetables are just tender. Serve vegetables topped with patties, sprinkle with coriander.

Serves 4.

- Pork patties can be prepared a day ahead.
- Storage: Covered, in refrigerator.
- Freeze: Uncooked pork patties suitable.
- Microwave: Not suitable.

Mat from Corso De' Fiori.

SWEET SOUR PORK SPARE RIBS

BABI MANIS DAN ASIN

6 (1kg) pork spare ribs
3 cloves garlic, crushed
1 teaspoon grated fresh galangal
2 tablespoons soy sauce
2 tablespoons rice wine
40g ghee
2 medium (300g) onions, sliced
2 teaspoons grated fresh
   galangal, extra
4 small fresh red chillies, chopped
1 cup (250ml) water
½ cup (125ml) plum sauce
2 tablespoons white vinegar
1 tablespoon white soy bean paste
1 tablespoon sugar
2 teaspoons soy sauce, extra
1 tablespoon cornflour
1 tablespoon water, extra
1 tablespoon chopped fresh
   coriander

1. Cut ribs in half, combine with garlic, galangal, sauce and wine in bowl; cover, refrigerate 2 hours. Drain, reserve marinade.

2. Heat 2 teaspoons ghee in pan, add ribs in batches, cook until well browned; remove from pan. Heat remaining ghee in same pan, add onions, extra galangal and chillies, cook, stirring, until onions are soft. Return ribs to pan.

3. Add reserved marinade, water, plum sauce, vinegar, soy bean paste, sugar and extra soy sauce, simmer, uncovered, about 30 minutes, stirring occasionally, or until ribs are tender. Stir in blended cornflour and extra water, stir until mixture boils and thickens. Sprinkle with coriander.

Serves 4.

- Recipe can be made an hour ahead.
- Storage: Covered, in refrigerator.
- Freeze: Suitable.
- Microwave: Not suitable.

Plate on stand from Accoutrement; fabric from Java Bazaar.

MEATBALL CURRY

KARI BERGEDEL

60g ghee
2 medium (300g) onions, chopped
1 clove garlic, crushed
1 tablespoon grated fresh ginger
½ teaspoon ground turmeric
½ teaspoon chilli powder
1 teaspoon garam masala
2 medium (260g) tomatoes,
    roughly chopped
1 tablespoon chopped fresh mint

MEATBALLS
750g minced beef
¼ cup chopped fresh coriander
1 medium (150g) onion, chopped
1 tablespoon grated fresh ginger
2 cloves garlic, crushed
½ teaspoon garam masala
1 small fresh red chilli,
    seeded, chopped

3. Meatballs: Combine all ingredients in bowl; mix well. Roll level tablespoons of mixture into balls.

Serves 4 to 6.

- Recipe can be made a day ahead.
- Storage: Covered, in refrigerator.
- Freeze: Suitable.
- Microwave: Not suitable.

1. Heat ghee in pan, add meatballs in batches, cook, turning, until well browned; drain on absorbent paper.

2. Add onions, garlic and ginger to same pan, cook, stirring, until onions are soft. Add spices, cook, stirring, until fragrant. Stir in tomatoes and meatballs, cook, covered, about 20 minutes or until meatballs are tender. Stir in mint.

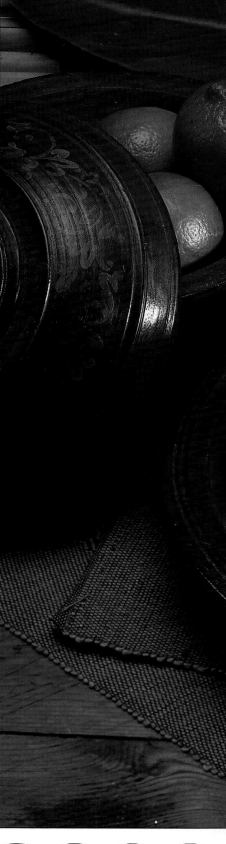

PORK AND POTATO CURRY

KARI BABI DAN UBI

1 stem fresh lemon grass, chopped
6 green shallots, chopped
2 cloves garlic, crushed
1 tablespoon chopped fresh turmeric
5 dried red chillies
1 tablespoon ground coriander
1 teaspoon fennel seeds
2 tablespoons vegetable oil
1kg diced pork
500g potatoes, chopped
2 cups (500ml) chicken stock
1 star anise
1 cinnamon stick
2 cloves
½ cup (125ml) coconut milk
1 tablespoon chopped fresh
   coriander

1. Blend or process lemon grass, shallots, garlic, turmeric, chillies, ground coriander and fennel seeds until well combined.

2. Heat half the oil in pan, add pork in batches, cook until well browned; remove from pan. Heat remaining oil in same pan, add blended lemon grass mixture, cook, stirring, until fragrant.

3. Return pork to pan, add potatoes, stock, star anise, cinnamon and cloves, simmer, covered, 30 minutes; remove lid, simmer further 20 minutes or until pork and potatoes are tender.

4. Add coconut milk, stir until heated through. Serve sprinkled with fresh coriander. Discard cinnamon and star anise before serving.

Serves 4 to 6.

- Recipe best made just before serving.
- Freeze: Not suitable.
- Microwave: Not suitable.

China from The Reject China Shop.

LAMB IN COCONUT MILK WITH TOMATOES

KARI KHEEMA KAMBING

4 dried red chillies, finely chopped
1 tablespoon ground coriander
1 tablespoon ground cumin
1 teaspoon ground anise
40g ghee
3 medium (450g) onions, sliced
2 teaspoons grated fresh turmeric
2 teaspoons grated fresh ginger
1 cinnamon stick
4 cloves
4 cardamom pods
500g minced lamb
1 cup (250ml) coconut milk
2 medium (260g) tomatoes, chopped

1. Add chillies, coriander, cumin and anise to dry pan, cook, stirring, until fragrant. Remove from pan.

2. Heat ghee in pan, add onions, cook, stirring, until soft. Add cooked spices, turmeric, ginger, cinnamon, cloves and cardamom, cook over low heat, stirring occasionally, 5 minutes.

3. Add mince, cook, stirring, until well browned, cover, simmer 15 minutes. Add coconut milk, cook, stirring, further 5 minutes or until most of the liquid is evaporated. Stir in tomatoes.

Serves 4.

- Recipe can be made a day ahead.
- Storage: Covered, in refrigerator.
- Freeze: Not suitable.
- Microwave: Suitable.

BRAISED PORK WITH EGGS

BABI TULANG MASAK TAYU

6 (1kg) pork spare ribs
¼ cup (60ml) vegetable oil
6 cloves garlic, crushed
2 teaspoons grated fresh ginger
1 cup (250ml) water
1½ tablespoons soy sauce
1 tablespoon chopped fresh
  coriander
8 green shallots, chopped
1 teaspoon cornflour
2 teaspoons water, extra
150g soft beancurd, cubed
3 hard-boiled eggs, halved

1. Trim bones and rind from pork, cut pork into 3cm pieces. Heat oil in pan, add garlic, cook, stirring, until lightly browned. Add ginger and pork, cook until pork is lightly browned all over.

2. Stir in water and soy sauce, simmer, uncovered, about 10 minutes or until pork is tender. Add coriander, shallots and blended cornflour and extra water, stir over heat until sauce boils and thickens. Stir in beancurd and eggs, simmer until heated through.

Serves 4 to 6.

■ Recipe best made just before serving.
■ Freeze: Not suitable.
■ Microwave: Not suitable.

Serving dish from Accoutrement.

LAMB WITH DHAL AND VEGETABLES

DALCHA

8 (1kg) lamb neck chops
1 cinnamon stick
2 star anise
1 teaspoon ground cardamom
3 fresh kaffir lime leaves
2 tablespoons lime juice
2 tablespoons soy sauce
1 cup (200g) red lentils
2 medium (600g) eggplants
200g green beans
2 tablespoons vegetable oil
1 large (200g) onion, sliced
6 small fresh red chillies, chopped
1 teaspoon grated fresh galangal
2 teaspoons mild curry powder
2 teaspoons cumin seeds
2 cups (500ml) water
270ml can coconut milk

1. Combine lamb, cinnamon, star anise, cardamom, leaves, juice and sauce in bowl; cover, refrigerate 1 hour.

2. Place lentils in bowl, cover well with water, cover, stand 30 minutes; drain, rinse. Cut eggplants into 2cm pieces. Cut beans into 5cm lengths.

3. Drain lamb, reserve marinade. Heat 2 teaspoons of the oil in pan, add lamb in batches, cook until well browned, remove from pan. Heat remaining oil in same pan, add onion, chillies, galangal, curry powder and seeds to pan, cook, stirring, until onion is soft. Return lamb to pan.

4. Stir in reserved marinade, water and coconut milk, simmer, covered, 30 minutes, stirring occasionally. Add lentils, eggplants and beans, simmer, covered, about 30 minutes or until lamb is tender. Discard cinnamon, star anise and lime leaves before serving.

Serves 4.

■ Recipe can be made an hour ahead.
■ Storage: Covered, in refrigerator.
■ Freeze: Not suitable.
■ Microwave: Not suitable.

CURRIED LAMB KEBABS

KEBAB KAMBING

Soak bamboo skewers in water for several hours or overnight to prevent them from burning.

650g lamb fillets
8cm (60g) fresh ginger, thinly sliced
12 baby (300g) onions, peeled, halved
60g ghee
1 medium (150g) onion, chopped
4 cloves garlic, crushed
2 small fresh red chillies,
**   finely chopped**
1 tablespoon mild curry powder
1 cup (250ml) water

1. Cut lamb into 3cm pieces. Thread lamb, ginger and baby onions alternately onto skewers.

2. Heat ghee in pan, add chopped onion, garlic and chillies, cook, stirring, until onion is soft. Add curry powder and water, stir until well combined.

3. Place kebabs in greased baking dish, pour over curry mixture, bake, uncovered, in hot oven about 15 minutes or until lamb is tender.

4. Remove kebabs from dish; keep warm. Boil sauce, uncovered, until reduced by half. Serve sauce spooned over kebabs.

Serves 4.

■ Recipe can be prepared a day ahead.
■ Freeze: Not suitable.
■ Microwave: Not suitable.

Plate from Accoutrement.

Sweets & Treats

CUCI MULUT

Malaysians traditionally serve tropical fresh fruits or little, mouth-watering sweets and pastries at the end of a meal or during afternoon tea. There is a stunning variety of intriguing fruits in Malaysia, such as the long, deeply ridged star fruit which forms a pretty star shape when cut in a cross-section, the mangosteen, sapodilla and the infamous, pungent durian. We have included two sauces for fruit here plus some beautifully rich sweets and desserts, based on coconut milk, palm sugar, rice, sago or pandan (screw pine leaf).

BANANA FRITTERS

GORENG PISANG

1 cup (150g) plain flour
¼ cup (35g) rice flour
1 tablespoon baking powder
1¼ cups (310ml) water, approximately
4 medium (800g) bananas
vegetable oil for deep-frying
2 tablespoons caster sugar

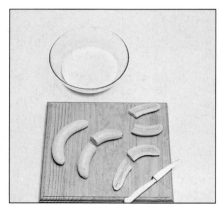

1. Sift flours and baking powder into bowl; gradually stir in enough water to mix to a smooth batter. Cut bananas in half lengthways then in half crossways.

2. Heat oil in pan. Dip bananas in batter, deep-fry in hot oil until lightly browned and crisp; drain on absorbent paper, sprinkle with sugar.

Serves 4.

▨ Recipe best made just before serving.
▨ Freeze: Not suitable.
▨ Microwave: Not suitable.

Bowl and tray from Corso De' Fiori.

SAGO PUDDING

SAGO DAN GULA MELAKA

1 litre (4 cups) water
1 cup (200g) sago (seed tapioca)
1 egg white
2 teaspoons brandy
1 teaspoon vanilla essence
yellow food colouring
½ cup (125ml) coconut cream

SYRUP
⅓ cup (90g) palm sugar
2 tablespoons water
2 teaspoons vanilla essence

1. Bring water to boil in pan, add sago, simmer, uncovered, about 20 minutes, stirring frequently, until sago is transparent and mixture is thick. Transfer sago mixture to bowl.

2. Beat egg white in small bowl with electric mixer until soft peaks form. Stir egg white, brandy, essence and a little colouring into sago mixture; mix well. Spread sago mixture evenly into 4 x ¾ cup (180ml) oiled moulds, smooth surface with wet hand; cover, refrigerate several hours or until set. Turn onto serving plates, serve with coconut cream and syrup.

3. Syrup: Combine all ingredients in small pan, stir over heat, without boiling, until sugar is dissolved and mixture is smooth; cool.

Serves 4.

■ Sago pudding and syrup can be made a day ahead.
■ Storage: Covered, separately, in refrigerator.
■ Freeze: Not suitable.
■ Microwave: Suitable.

Plate from Reject China Shop; tray and bowl from Corso De' Fiori.

CUSTARD TARTS

TAN TAT

1½ cups (225g) plain flour
2 tablespoons icing sugar mixture
170g cold butter, chopped
1 egg yolk
2 tablespoons iced water,
    approximately

CUSTARD
¾ cup (165g) sugar
1¼ cups (310ml) water
5 eggs, lightly beaten
½ cup (125ml) milk

1. Sift flour and icing sugar into bowl, rub in butter, add egg yolk and enough water to make ingredients cling together; wrap in plastic wrap, refrigerate 30 minutes.

2. Divide dough into 2 portions, roll each portion to 2mm thickness. Cut pastry into 8cm rounds. Line greased deep fluted tart tins (¼ cup (60ml) capacity) with pastry rounds.

3. Pour custard carefully into pastry cases until custard comes three-quarters of the way up the sides of pastry. Bake in hot oven 10 minutes, reduce heat to moderately hot, bake further 10 minutes or until custard is set.

4. Custard: Combine sugar and water in pan, stir over heat, without boiling, until sugar is dissolved; cool. Combine sugar syrup, eggs and milk in bowl, stir until well combined.

Makes about 30.

▨ Recipe best made close to serving.
▨ Freeze: Not suitable.
▨ Microwave: Not suitable.

Plate from Accoutrement.

PINEAPPLE TARTLETS

KUEH TAT NENAS

1¼ cups (185g) plain flour
¼ cup (35g) self-raising flour
¼ cup (55g) caster sugar
90g cold butter, chopped
1 egg, lightly beaten
1 tablespoon iced water,
    approximately
⅓ cup (80ml) pineapple jam,
    approximately
milk

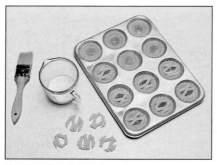

4. Brush edges of tartlets with milk, top with lattice rounds, press lightly, brush with milk. Bake in moderate oven about 15 minutes or until lightly browned, loosen tartlets in pans; cool.

Makes 36.

■ Recipe can be made 3 days ahead.
■ Storage: Airtight container.
■ Freeze: Suitable.
■ Microwave: Not suitable.

1. Sift flours and sugar into large bowl, rub in butter. Add egg and enough water to make ingredients cling together. Press dough into a ball, knead on floured surface until smooth; cover, refrigerate 30 minutes.

2. Lightly grease 3 x 12-hole shallow patty pan trays. Roll out two-thirds of the pastry to 2mm thickness, cut out 36 x 5.5cm rounds. Line pans with pastry rounds; fill with half a teaspoon of jam.

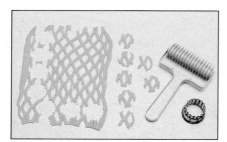

3. Roll remaining pastry to 3mm thickness. Roll a lattice cutter along the length of pastry, carefully ease open to give lattice effect. Cut out 36 x 4.5cm rounds.

Fabric and carving from Java Bazaar.

BLACK STICKY RICE

BUBOR PULOT HITAM

1 cup (200g) black glutinous rice
2 cups (500ml) coconut milk
⅓ cup (90g) palm sugar
coconut cream

1. Place rice in bowl, cover well with water, cover, stand overnight; drain.

2. Add rice to pan of boiling water, simmer, uncovered, about 15 minutes or until tender; drain.

3. Combine rice, coconut milk and sugar in pan, simmer, uncovered, stirring occasionally, about 15 minutes, or until thickened to porridge-like consistency. Serve drizzled with a little coconut cream.

Serves 6.

- Recipe best made just before serving.
- Freeze: Not suitable.
- Microwave: Suitable.

Bowls from Reject China Shop; tray from Corso De' Fiori.

TAPIOCA BALLS

ONDE ONDE

2¾ cups (350g) glutinous rice flour
1½ tablespoons tapioca flour
½ cup (135g) palm sugar
1 tablespoon caster sugar
1 cup (250ml) water
½ teaspoon pandan extract
¾ cup (60g) coconut

1. Blend or process flours and sugars until well combined.

2. Combine water and pandan extract in bowl; mix well. Add flour mixture to pandan mixture to form a firm paste. Roll tablespoons of paste into balls.

3. Cook paste balls in batches in boiling water about 5 minutes or until they float to the surface. Remove from water with slotted spoon, roll in coconut.

Makes about 30.

- Recipe best made on day of serving.
- Storage: Covered, at room temperature.
- Freeze: Not suitable.
- Microwave: Not suitable.

PANDAN CHIFFON CAKE

KUEH PANDAN

Tube pans are available from specialty cookware shops. It is important not to grease pan; the delicate cake mixture needs the surface to cling to during baking and cooling. The pan has small feet to allow cake to cool suspended.

8 eggs, separated
1¼ cups (275g) caster sugar
¾ cup (180ml) vegetable oil
1 teaspoon vanilla essence
¾ cup (180ml) coconut milk
¼ teaspoon pandan extract
1 cup (150g) self-raising flour
1 egg white
1 teaspoon cream of tartar

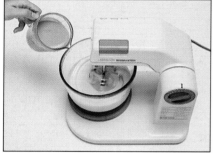

1. Beat egg yolks, sugar, oil and essence in small bowl with electric mixer until combined. Beat in combined coconut milk and pandan extract.

2. Sift flour 3 times into large bowl, make well in centre, whisk egg mixture into flour.

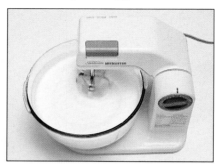

3. Beat all egg whites in large bowl with electric mixer until frothy, add cream of tartar, beat until firm peaks form.

4. Fold egg whites into flour mixture in 2 batches using balloon whisk.

5. Carefully pour mixture into 21cm ungreased tube pan; pull skewer through mixture to disperse bubbles. Bake in moderately hot oven about 45 minutes or until cake feels springy to touch. Gently invert pan on bench. Do not move or bump pan until cake is completely cold. Run a spatula around side of pan to release cake.

Serves 10.

▦ Recipe can be made a day ahead.
▦ Storage: Airtight container.
▦ Freeze: Not suitable.
▦ Microwave: Not suitable.

Setting from Morris Home & Garden Wares.

TROPICAL FRUIT WITH TWO CITRUS SAUCES

BUAH BUAHAN DAN SOS

1 medium (430g) mango
2 medium (300g) star fruit
1 medium (1.25kg) pineapple
1 medium (200g) banana
1 medium (1.25kg) pawpaw
½ medium (1.4kg) honeydew melon

LEMON LIQUEUR SAUCE
½ cup (100g) firmly packed
  brown sugar
⅓ cup (80ml) lemon juice
⅓ (80ml) cup water
1 tablespoon Cointreau
5 cloves

CARAMEL ORANGE SAUCE
2 tablespoons water
½ cup (110g) caster sugar
¾ cup (180ml) orange juice
1 tablespoon Grand Marnier
5 cloves

1. Holding mango upright, cut down either side of stone to obtain 2 mango cheeks. Make 3 diagonal cuts into flesh of 1 cheek, turn mango and make 3 more cuts at right angles to the first cuts. Invert mango, cut pieces neatly from skin. Repeat with other mango cheek.

2. Cut star fruit, pineapple and banana into 2cm slices. Brush banana with a little lemon juice. Cut pawpaw and melon into 3cm pieces. Serve fruit with sauces.

3. Lemon Liqueur Sauce: Combine all ingredients in pan, stir over heat, without boiling, until sugar is dissolved; cool.

4. Caramel Orange Sauce: Combine water and sugar in pan, stir over heat, without boiling, until sugar is dissolved. Bring to boil, boil, uncovered, without stirring, until golden brown. Stir in remaining ingredients, stir until toffee is dissolved; cool.

Serves 6.

■ Fruit best prepared just before serving. Sauces can be made a day ahead.
■ Storage: Covered, in refrigerator.
■ Freeze: Not suitable.
■ Microwave: Not suitable.

Glossary

Here are some terms, names and alternatives to help everyone use and understand our recipes perfectly.

ANISE, GROUND: one of the main spices in five-spice powder; has a licorice flavour.

BAKING POWDER: is a raising agent consisting of an alkali and an acid; mostly made from bicarbonate of soda and cream of tartar in proportions of 1 level teaspoon of cream of tartar to $\frac{1}{2}$ level teaspoon bicarbonate of soda. This is equivalent to 2 teaspoons baking powder.

BANANA LEAVES: can be ordered from fruit and vegetable stores. Usually, 1 leaf is cut into about 10 pieces. Cut with a sharp knife close to the main stem then immerse in hot water so that leaves will be pliable.

BAMBOO SHOOTS: the young tender shoots of bamboo plants, are available in cans. Mainly used to add texture to food.

BEANCURD: also known as tofu. It is made from boiled, crushed soya beans to give a type of milk. A coagulant is added, much like the process of cheese making. Beancurd is easily digested, nutritious and has a slightly nutty flavour. Buy it as fresh as possible; keep any leftover beancurd in refrigerator under water, which must be changed daily. Its flavour is delicate and texture smooth and soft like baked custard.

Soft: mainly used in soups.

Fried: cubes of soft beancurd deep-fried until surface is brown and crusty and the inside almost dry. Available in packets.

Clockwise from top left: Fried beancurd, beancurd sheets, firm beancurd, soft beancurd.

Firm: made by compressing beancurd to remove most of the water. Used in a variety of dishes.

Sheets: beancurd dried into thin skins, sold in sheets and used as wrappers. Immerse sheet in bowl of cold water, stand 1 minute, place on a towel and cut into required lengths. If beancurd is not soaked the sheet will crumble.

BELACAN: dried shrimp paste sold in slabs or flat cakes. No real substitute, the closest being shrimp paste.

Belacan.

BICARBONATE OF SODA: baking soda.

BREADCRUMBS:

Stale: use 1 or 2-day-old bread made into crumbs by grating, blending or processing.

BROAD BEANS: available fresh, frozen and dried.

BUTTER: use salted or unsalted (also called sweet) butter; 125g is equal to 1 stick butter.

CALAMARI: a type of squid.

CANDLENUTS: a hard nut, used to thicken curries in Malaysia and Indonesia. Almonds, brazil nuts or macadamias can be substituted.

CARDAMOM: spice with an exotic fragrance; bought in pod, seed or ground form.

CHICKPEAS: garbanzos.

CHILLIES: use rubber gloves when chopping fresh chillies as they can burn your skin.

Powder: the Asian variety is the hottest and is made from ground chillies; it can be used as a substitute for fresh chillies in the proportions of $\frac{1}{2}$ teaspoon ground chilli powder to 1 medium chopped fresh chilli.

Dried: whole chillies.

CHILLI SAUCE: we used a hot Chinese variety. It consists of chillies, salt and vinegar. We used it sparingly; you can increase it to taste.

CHILLI SAUCE, SWEET: we used a mild sauce made from red chillies, sugar, garlic, salt and vinegar.

CHINESE SAUSAGES: highly spiced, bright red, thin pork sausages. Because of the high spice content the meat is preserved and can be kept at room temperature.

From left: Chinese sausages, fish balls.

COCONUT: use desiccated coconut unless otherwise specified.

Cream: available in cans and cartons.

Milk: available in cans from supermarkets.

Candlenuts.

COINTREAU: an orange-flavoured liqueur.

COOKING SALT: a coarse salt (not the same as fine table salt).

CORNFLOUR: cornstarch.

CREAMED CORN: canned product.

CREAM OF TARTAR: an acid which, when combined with an alkali such as bicarbonate of soda, acts as a raising agent. It is one of the ingredients of baking powder.

CURRY LEAVES: are available fresh or dried and have a mild curry flavour.

CURRY POWDER: a convenient combination of powdered spices, consisting of chilli, coriander, cumin, fennel, fenugreek and turmeric.

CUTTLEFISH: generally smaller than squid with a thicker body, hard cuttlebone and ink sac.

DAIKON RADISH: is a large, white-skinned, mild-flavoured Japanese radish. A vegetable of the turnip family.

DRIED ANCHOVIES: available in packets from Asian food stores.

DRIED SHRIMPS: dried salted baby prawns.

Clockwise from top right: Dried shrimps, packaged fried onions, dried anchovies.

EGG NOODLES, FRESH: made from wheat flour and eggs; varying in thickness from fine strands to pieces as thick as a shoelace.

Clockwise from left: Fresh egg noodles, rice vermicelli noodles, fresh yellow noodles.

FENNEL: has a slight aniseed taste whether fresh, ground or in seed form. Fennel seeds are a component of curry powder.

FISH BALLS: are made from pounded fish paste and bought, fresh or frozen, in packets from Asian specialty stores.

FISH SAUCE: made from the liquid drained from salted, fermented anchovies. It has a strong smell and taste; use sparingly.

FIVE SPICE POWDER: a pungent mixture of ground spices which include cinnamon, cloves, fennel, star anise and Szechwan peppers.

FLOUR:

Glutinous rice: made from ground glutinous rice. More elastic than ordinary flour. It becomes almost clear and sticky when cooked.

Plain: all-purpose flour.

Rice: flour made from ground rice.

Self-raising: substitute plain (all-purpose) flour and baking powder in the proportions of 1 cup (150g) plain flour to 2 level teaspoons baking powder. Sift together several times before using.

Tapioca: flour made from the fleshy root of cassava or manioc, a tropical plant.

FRENCH SHALLOTS: very small onion with brown skin. It grows in clusters, and has a strong onion and garlic flavour.

FRESH HERBS: we have specified when to use fresh or dried herbs. We used dried (not ground) herbs in the proportions of 1:4 for fresh herbs, e.g., 1 teaspoon dried herbs instead of 4 teaspoons (1 tablespoon) chopped fresh herbs.

From left: Mint, coriander and Vietnamese mint.

FRIED ONIONS, PACKAGED: crisp, fried onion flakes. Available from Asian food stores.

GALANGAL: a member of the ginger family, available dried, ground and fresh. Scrape away skin and grate, chop or slice as required.

GARAM MASALA: often used in Indian cooking, this spice combines cardamom, cinnamon, cloves, coriander, cumin and nutmeg in varying proportions. Sometimes pepper is used to make a hot variation.

GHEE: a pure butter fat, it can be heated to high temperatures without burning because of the lack of salts and milk solids.

GINGER:

Fresh, green or root ginger: scrape away skin and grate, chop or slice as required. To preserve fresh, peeled ginger, cover with dry sherry in a jar and refrigerate.

Clockwise from left: Fresh turmeric, fresh galangal, fresh lemon grass, fresh ginger.

GOW GEES PASTRY: wonton wrappers, spring roll or egg pastry sheets can be substituted.

Clockwise from top left: Wonton wrappers, gow gees pastry rounds, spring roll wrappers.

GRAND MARNIER: an orange-flavoured liqueur.

GREEN SHALLOTS: also known as scallions and green onions. Do not confuse these with the small French shallots.

HOI SIN SAUCE: is a thick, sweet, Chinese barbecue sauce made from salted black beans, onions and garlic.

HONEYDEW MELON: is very sweet, with crisp, bright green flesh.

KAFFIR LIME LEAVES: also known as citrus or lime leaves, available in fresh and dried form. They give a unique flavour to Malaysian food.

From left: Kaffir lime leaves, dried curry leaves.

KUMARA: orange-coloured sweet potato.

Kumara.

LAMINGTON PAN: 20cm x 30cm rectangular cake pan, 3cm deep.

LEMON GRASS: available from Asian food stores. The thick stem, not the leafy part, is used, bruised or chopped before using.

LENTILS: dried pulses. There are many different varieties, usually identified and named after their colour.

MUTTON: the meat from a mature sheep.

OIL:

Sesame: an oil made from roasted, crushed white sesame seeds. Do not use for frying.

Vegetable: we used polyunsaturated vegetable oil.

OYSTER SAUCE: a rich brown sauce made from oysters cooked in salt and soy sauce, then thickened with starches.

PANDAN EXTRACT: Screw pine leaves are pounded and juice extracted.

Pandan extract.

PLUM SAUCE: a dipping sauce made of plums, sugar, chillies and spices.

PRAWNS: shrimps.

RICE:

Glutinous, white and black: a variety of rice which tends to stick together when cooked.

Long-grain: elongated grains.

Short-grain: about half the length of long-grain rice, but thicker.

Clockwise from top: Black glutinous rice, white glutinous rice, short-grain rice, long-grain rice.

SALTED BLACK BEANS: fermented, salted soya beans. Canned and dried black beans can be substituted. Drain and rinse canned variety; soak and rinse dried variety. Leftover beans will keep for months in an airtight container in the refrigerator. Mash beans when cooking to release flavour.

SAMBAL OELEK (also ulek or olek): a paste of ground chillies and salt.

SAGO: also sold as seed tapioca. Tapioca can be used as a substitute for sago; it will need more cooking.

SNOW PEAS: also known as mange tout (eat all).

SOY/SOYA:

Bean cake, fried: from Asian food stores; has firm texture.

Paste, white: also known as miso. Made from preserved soya beans, rice, malt, salt and water.

Sauce: made from fermented soya beans.

From left: Soy bean paste, fried soya bean cake.

SPINACH:

English: a soft-leafed vegetable, more delicate in taste than silverbeet (spinach); young silverbeet can be substituted.

Clockwise from front left: Choy sum, baby bok choy, Chinese cabbage, English spinach, bean sprouts.

SPRING ROLL WRAPPERS: thin white sheets of pastry, sold frozen. Thaw before using. Unused wrappers can be stored in the freezer.

SQUID: is a type of mollusc; also known as calamari.

STAR ANISE: the dried star-shaped fruit of an evergreen tree. It has an aniseed flavour and is used sparingly in Asian cooking.

Star anise.

STOCK: 1 cup (250ml) stock is the equivalent of 1 cup (250ml) water plus 1 crumbled stock cube (or 1 teaspoon stock powder). If you prefer to make your own fresh stock, see recipes on following page.

STAR FRUIT: also known as carambola and belimbing (a smaller variety).

SUGAR: we used coarse granulated table sugar, also known as crystal sugar, unless otherwise specified.

Brown: a soft, fine, granulated sugar containing molasses.

Caster: also known as superfine; is fine granulated table sugar.

Palm: very fine sugar from the coconut palm. It is sold in cakes, also known as gula jawa, gula melaka and jaggery. Palm sugar can be substituted with brown or black sugar.

TAMARIND:

Concentrate: a thick liquid made from the acid-tasting fruit of the tamarind tree.

Paste: is available in packets from Asian food stores. Prepare as specified in our recipes to remove seeds.

From left: Tamarind paste, tamarind concentrate.

TOFU: also known as beancurd.

Palm sugar.

TOMATO:

Paste: a concentrated tomato puree used in flavouring soups, stews, sauces and casseroles, etc.

Sauce: tomato ketchup.

TURMERIC: available fresh and ground. A member of the ginger family, its root is dried and ground, giving the rich yellow powder which gives curry its characteristic colour; it is not hot in flavour.

VANILLA ESSENCE: we used imitation vanilla essence, also known as extract.

VERMICELLI: very fine rice noodles.

VINEGAR: we used both white and brown malt vinegar.

Rice: milder in flavour than fruit and wine vinegars; it is light golden in colour.

White: made from spirit of cane sugar.

Wine: made from wine, often flavoured with herbs, spices, fruit, etc.

YAM BEAN: tuberous root with crisp white flesh and fresh flavour. Can be eaten uncooked.

Clockwise from left: Yam bean, daikon radish and okra.

YELLOW NOODLES: made from wheat flour, salt and vegetable oil; varying in thickness.

MAKE YOUR OWN STOCK

BEEF STOCK
2kg meaty beef bones
2 medium (300g) onions
2 sticks celery, chopped
2 medium (250g) carrots, chopped
3 bay leaves
2 teaspoons black peppercorns
5 litres (20 cups) water
3 litres (12 cups) water, extra

Place bones and unpeeled chopped onions in baking dish. Bake in hot oven about 1 hour or until bones and onions are well browned. Transfer bones and onions to large pan, add celery, carrots, bay leaves, peppercorns and water, simmer, uncovered, 3 hours. Add extra water, simmer, uncovered, further 1 hour; strain. Makes about 2.5 litres (10 cups).
- Stock can be made 4 days ahead.
- Storage: Covered, in refrigerator.
- Freeze: Suitable.
- Microwave: Not suitable.

CHICKEN STOCK
2kg chicken bones
2 medium (300g) onions, chopped
2 sticks celery, chopped
2 medium (250g) carrots, chopped
3 bay leaves
2 teaspoons black peppercorns
5 litres (20 cups) water

Combine all ingredients in large pan, simmer, uncovered, 2 hours; strain. Makes about 2.5 litres (10 cups).
- Stock can be made 4 days ahead.
- Storage: Covered, in refrigerator.
- Freeze: Suitable.
- Microwave: Not suitable.

FISH STOCK
1.5kg fish bones
3 litres (12 cups) water
1 medium (150g) onion, chopped
2 sticks celery, chopped
2 bay leaves
1 teaspoon black peppercorns

Combine all ingredients in large pan, simmer, uncovered, 20 minutes; strain. Makes about 2.5 litres (10 cups).
- Stock can be made 4 days ahead.
- Storage: Covered, in refrigerator.
- Freeze: Suitable.
- Microwave: Not suitable.

VEGETABLE STOCK
1 large (180g) carrot, chopped
1 large (350g) parsnip, chopped
2 medium (300g) onions, chopped
6 sticks celery, chopped
4 bay leaves
2 teaspoons black peppercorns
3 litres (12 cups) water

Combine all ingredients in large pan, simmer, uncovered, 1½ hours; strain. Makes about 1.25 litres (5 cups).
- Stock can be made 4 days ahead.
- Storage: Covered, in refrigerator.
- Freeze: Suitable.
- Microwave: Suitable.

Index

QUICK CONVERSION GUIDE

Wherever you live in the world you can use our recipes with the help of our easy-to-follow conversions for all your cooking needs. These conversions are approximate only. The difference between the exact and approximate conversions of liquid and dry measures amounts to only a teaspoon or two, and will not make any difference to your cooking results.

MEASURING EQUIPMENT

The difference between measuring cups internationally is minimal within 2 or 3 teaspoons' difference. (For the record, 1 Australian metric measuring cup will hold approximately 250ml.) The most accurate way of measuring dry ingredients is to weigh them. When measuring liquids use a clear glass or plastic jug with metric markings.

In this book we use metric measuring cups and spoons approved by Standards Australia.

● a graduated set of four cups for measuring dry ingredients; the sizes are marked on the cups.
● a graduated set of four spoons for measuring dry and liquid ingredients; the amounts are marked on the spoons.
● 1 TEASPOON: 5ml.
● 1 TABLESPOON: 20ml.

NOTE: NZ, CANADA, USA AND UK ALL USE 15ml TABLESPOONS.
ALL CUP AND SPOON MEASUREMENTS ARE LEVEL.

DRY MEASURES

METRIC	IMPERIAL
15g	½oz
30g	1oz
60g	2oz
90g	3oz
125g	4oz (¼lb)
155g	5oz
185g	6oz
220g	7oz
250g	8oz (½lb)
280g	9oz
315g	10oz
345g	11oz
375g	12oz (¾lb)
410g	13oz
440g	14oz
470g	15oz
500g	16oz (1lb)
750g	24oz (1½lb)
1kg	32oz (2lb)

LIQUID MEASURES

METRIC	IMPERIAL
30ml	1 fluid oz
60ml	2 fluid oz
100ml	3 fluid oz
125ml	4 fluid oz
150ml	5 fluid oz (¼ pint/1 gill)
190ml	6 fluid oz
250ml	8 fluid oz
300ml	10 fluid oz (½ pint)
500ml	16 fluid oz
600ml	20 fluid oz (1 pint)
1000ml (1 litre)	1¾ pints

WE USE LARGE EGGS WITH AN AVERAGE WEIGHT OF 60g

HELPFUL MEASURES

METRIC	IMPERIAL
3mm	⅛in
6mm	¼in
1cm	½in
2cm	¾in
2.5cm	1in
5cm	2in
6cm	2½in
8cm	3in
10cm	4in
13cm	5in
15cm	6in
18cm	7in
20cm	8in
23cm	9in
25cm	10in
28cm	11in
30cm	12in (1ft)

HOW TO MEASURE

When using the graduated metric measuring cups, it is important to shake the dry ingredients loosely into the required cup. Do not tap the cup on the bench, or pack the ingredients into the cup unless otherwise directed. Level top of cup with knife. When using graduated metric measuring spoons, level top of spoon with knife. When measuring liquids in the jug, place jug on flat surface, check for accuracy at eye level.

OVEN TEMPERATURES

These oven temperatures are only a guide; we've given you the lower degree of heat. Always check the manufacturer's manual.

	C° (Celsius)	F° (Fahrenheit)	Gas Mark
Very slow	120	250	1
Slow	150	300	2
Moderately slow	160	325	3
Moderate	180	350	4
Moderately hot	190	375	5
Hot	200	400	6
Very hot	230	450	7

TWO GREAT OFFERS FROM THE AWW HOME LIBRARY

Here's the perfect way to keep your Home Library books in order, clean and within easy reach. More than a dozen books fit into this smart silver grey vinyl folder. PRICE: Australia $9.95; elsewhere $19.95; prices include postage and handling. To order your holder, see the details below.

All recipes in the AWW Home Library are created using Australia's unique system of metric cups and spoons. While it is relatively easy for overseas readers to make any minor conversions required, it is easier still to own this durable set of Australian cups and spoons (photographed). PRICE : Australia: $5.95; New Zealand: $A8.00; elsewhere: $A9.95; prices include postage & handling.
This offer is available in all countries.

TO ORDER YOUR METRIC MEASURING SET OR BOOK HOLDER:

PHONE: Have your credit card details ready. **Sydney:** (02) 260 0035; **elsewhere in Australia:** 008 252 515 (free call, Mon-Fri, 9am-5pm) or *FAX* your order to (02) 267 4363 or *MAIL* your order by photocopying or cutting out and completing the coupon below.

PAYMENT: **Australian residents:** We accept the credit cards listed, money orders and cheques. **Overseas residents:** We accept the credit cards listed, drafts in $A drawn on an Australian bank, also English, New Zealand and U.S. cheques in the currency of the country of issue.
Credit card charges are at the exchange rate current at the time of payment.

Please photocopy and complete coupon and fax or send to:
AWW Home Library Reader Offer, ACP Direct, PO Box 7036, Sydney 2001.

❏ Metric Measuring Set   ❏ Holder
Please indicate number(s) required.

Mr/Mrs/Ms _____

Address _____

_____

Postcode_____ Country_____
Ph: (   ) _____ Bus. Hour:_____
I enclose my cheque/money order for $ _____ payable to ACP Direct

OR: please charge my:

❏ Bankcard ❏ Visa ❏ MasterCard ❏ Diners Club ❏ Amex

▢▢▢▢▢▢▢▢▢▢▢▢▢▢▢▢▢▢▢▢ Exp. Date ___/__

Cardholder's signature_____

(Please allow up to 30 days for delivery within Australia. Allow up to 6 weeks for overseas deliveries.)
Both offers expire 30/12/94.

AWRB94